⚡FOUND⚡

Davy Rothbart

FOUND

Funny! Tragic! Random!
Notes picked up from the street

CASSELL
ILLUSTRATED

A CASSELL BOOK

An Hachette Livre UK Company

First published in the UK 2008 by
Cassell Illustrated, a division of
Octopus Publishing Group Ltd.
2-4 Heron Quays,
London E14 4JP

Text, design and layout © 2008 Octopus Publishing Group Ltd.

A CIP catalogue record for this book
is available from the British Library.
ISBN-13: 978-1-844-03657-8

10 9 8 7 6 5 4 3 2 1

Project Editor: Fiona Kellagher
Layout: Laura Price
Production: Caroline Alberti

Commissioning Editor: Laura Price
Creative Director: Geoff Fennell
Publisher: Mathew Clayton

Printed in China

Late one snowy night in Chicago I left my friend's apartment and went out to my car. On the windshield I found a note intended for someone else, a guy named Mario.

Since grade school I've been collecting notes, letters, photographs, and other stuff I found on the ground. It always amazed me how powerfully I could connect with a person I'd never met just by reading a half-page love letter left behind on a park bench or the city bus. When I discovered Amber's note to Mario, I was so moved by its blend of anger and longing that I knew I needed to find a way to share it with the world. A few days later, driving from one small Mississippi town to the next, I had an idea: Why not create a magazine and publish Amber's note, along with the rest of the incredible finds my friends and I had turned up over the years?

> Mario,
> I fucking hate you you said you had to work then whys your car HERE at <u>HER</u> place ??
> You're a fucking LIAR. I hate you
> I fucking hate you
> Amber
> PS Page me later

As I traveled around the country the next few months, I passed out flyers inviting folks to send in stuff they'd found. At first, I didn't hear anything. Then, suddenly, I did. Found notes came in from as far away as Alaska and Bangladesh. They were by turns beautiful, hilarious, and heartbreaking. Once I'd gathered a decent stack of material and combed through my own collection of found stuff, my friend Jason Bitner and I went to work for three nights cutting and pasting with scissors and tape and put together the first issue of *FOUND Magazine*.

The response completely stunned and overwhelmed me. New Found stuff began pouring in from all over the globe. I had no idea so many people shared my fascination with found stuff and other people's lives. Folks have written in who've been collecting these types of treasures since before my parents were born. And then a lot of people — particularly in small, rural towns — have said "All these years I've been picking up stuff off the street and everyone here thinks I'm a freak. But now I see that I am not alone!" I love that. It's exciting to sense an invisible community emerging from the shadows and finding each other.

But what I love most about this project is that everyone can play. People who've never been into finding things before have told me that they've begun to look at the world in a new way. We've gotten finds from dozens of countries and every state in the U.S. Finds arrived one week from both Iceland and Greenland, which I thought was kind of a coup. Kids as young as 6 years old have sent in their finds.

I ask folks to name their finds, just as they'd name a painting or a song or a story they'd written. Picking a note up from the ground — something that everyone else has walked past and seen as trash — seems to me an equally noble act of creation. We're always careful to give credit to the person who's found each item; they deserve recognition for rescuing their find from the gutter and giving it new life.

Found notes and letters open up the entire range of human experience; they offer a shortcut directly into people's minds and hearts. We often feel most alive when we're glimpsing someone at their most honest and raw. I think that's because when we read these notes, there's a powerful moment of recognition; we see another person – maybe someone very different from us — experiencing the same thoughts and feelings and emotions that we've experienced. It's startling and it's magical. Suddenly, we feel connected to this person we've never met before and probably never will, and in turn, to all people. The idea that we all share the same universal emotions and experiences — that we're all connected – strikes me as profoundly beautiful.

Some finds feel incomplete: They hint at a story but withhold important details. The things you don't know are often as fascinating as the things you do. Part of the joy of finding something is the imaginative process that ensues, trying to piece together a narrative that will make sense of things. There are questions to be answered: Who wrote this? What do some of these strange, cryptic phrases mean exactly? How did this thing end up here? Was this note trashed by the person who wrote it or the person who received it? It's up to the finder to guess at these riddles, knowing they will never truly be solved.

Folks ask me where the best places to find stuff are. Certainly, some spots are more fertile than others. I like sidewalks and bushes, all forms of public transportation, elementary school playgrounds, the recycling bins at Kinko's and university computer centers. While I appreciate the efforts of determined finders who prowl through Dumpsters looking for troves of abandoned letters, I think it's a mistake for folks to believe that you have to go far out of your way to find things. It's more a matter of simply keeping your eyes peeled during your everyday wanderings through the world. On your way to work, on your way to school, be aware of what's around you. And if you see a piece of paper lying there with writing on it, take a second and a half to pick it up and check it out. Four out of five notes you pick up might not be anything too interesting, but that fifth one will always be a real gem.

I always tend to get consumed with my little daily problems. I worry about girls and money and what the hell I did with my dang keys. Looking for found stuff is good for me because it brings me back to the present moment. I'm brought out of my own head and into the world around me. I start listening to conversations between strangers, gazing at people's faces, feeling them. Even if I don't find any wonderful notes on the ground, my day is far richer for having deeply experienced my surroundings.

Thank you *so much* for peeping this book and becoming a part of this. On the pages that follow is stuff people found. I implore you to join in — finding is fun! I can't wait to check out what *you* turn up.

All right, enough bullshit, let's get this fuckin' party started. Read on, my friends, read on — and for goodness sake, keep your eyes to the ground and send in your finds!

Much love, and peace out for now—

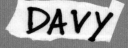
DAVY

2

Amos—
Last night was terrible! I'm
so mad at you. I thought we
agreed about that thing you
do... you know? It's not
kinky — it's GROSS!!! You
need to get over this phase of
yours. If you don't, well then
you can just sleep ALONE!
I'm sorry that I couldn't say this
to your face, but I can't bare
to look @ you right now. I
have to go, I have calculus
next period. Don't call me
I don't want to talk to you
or see you later this it's
get over this it's
really damaging
our sex life
— Mary

AMOS' GROSS PHASE
FOUND by Melissa Brown

8

RON RELATED
FOUND by Mark Stevens

"I found this note in my front yard, folded up, soggy and dirty. On the outside of the note it said, 'Read Last.'" **Mark**

MAY 23, 1996

DEAR RON,

THE LONGER I THINK ABOUT WHAT I'M DOING THE SICKER I FEEL. RON I'M SORRY BUT I DON'T ~~THINK~~ THAT WE SHOULD CONTINUE TO HAVE A RELATIONSHIP TOGETHER; AT LEAST NOT AS ~~XXX~~ A COUPLE. I LOVE YOU BUT THINGS HAVE NOT BEEN THE SAME SINCE WE FOUND OUT THAT WE WERE RELATED. IF YOU NO LONGER WANT TO SPEAK TO ME BECAUSE OF THIS, I WILL UNDERSTAND. I WILL STILL COME VISIT YOU ON SUNDAYS IF YOU LIKE, I JUST DON'T KNOW WHAT TO SAY TO YOU.

LOVE ALWAYS,
ALISHA

SEPT 16, 95

"CHICO PUNK SPONGE" "THIEF" "TEARDROP" "SHIT STAIN"

PETER! THANKS SO MUCH. FOR STOPPING BY FOR FIVE MONTHS AND SPONGING. LEAVING SPUNK TRACKS ON MY CLEAN BLANKETS. LEAVING EVERYTHING NAMELY BILL'S UNPAID. TAKING MY STEREO WATCH CASSETTE TAPE. I KNOW IT'S A HORRIBLE THING HAVING PEOPLE GIVE YOU FOOD WHEN YOUR HONGRY, SHELTER, TABBACO, MONEY. HOW COULD I HAVE BEEN SO CRUEL.

HEY I KNOW THE CLOTHES I GAVE YOU JUST WERNT COOL ENOUGH. I KNOW CLEANING UP AFTER YOU WASNT GOOD ENOUGH. I SHOULD HAVE CLEANED YOUR ROOM WASHED YOUR CLOTHES AND WIPED YOUR STINKING ASS. AT LEAST THAT WAY MAYBE YOUR SPONGE FREINTS COULD STAND YOUR STINK!

LET'S NOT FORGET BRINGING A WONDERFUL 15 YEAR OLD FAT CHICK RUNAWAY TO OUR PLACE. OF COURSE HIDING HER HERE HAS BROUGHT THE COP'S. THE NEIGHBORS ESPECIALY APPRECIATED THE COP'S BUSTING IN TO THEIR PLACE. THEY THINK SO MUCH OF YOU NOW! GOSH GOLLY WE ALL DO!

HUGS AND KISSES Chad YOUR FREIND FOR LIFE!

LIFE LESSON
FOUND by Alexis Coren

EXPECTATION
=
DISAPO

Kings & Queens Inn®
If this is
still here, they
didn't make the bed
after I slept in it.
yuck
Our Guests are Royalty.

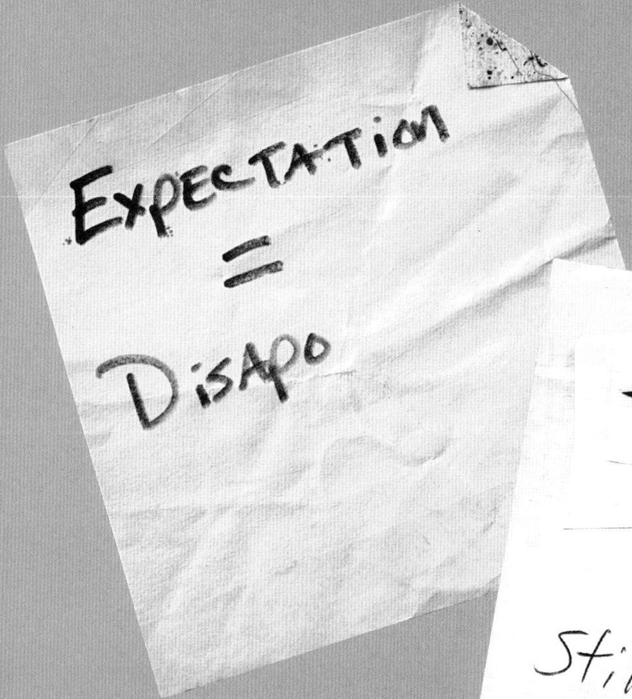

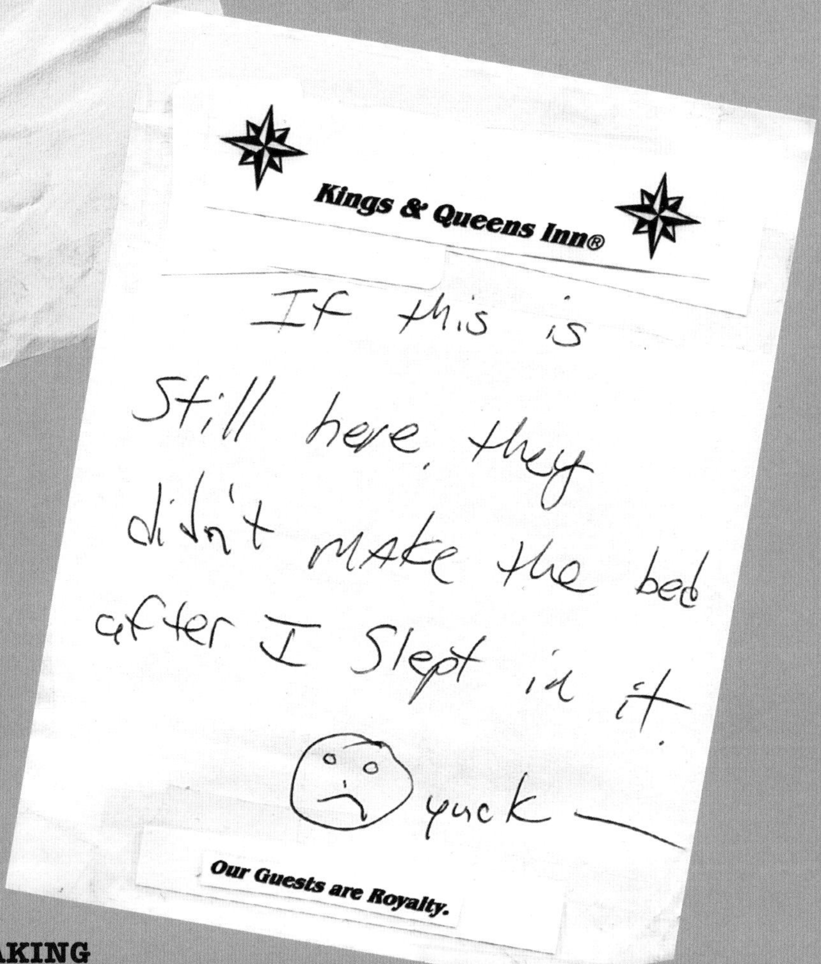

BED MAKING
FOUND by Jen Shaw

THE 2ND FAX

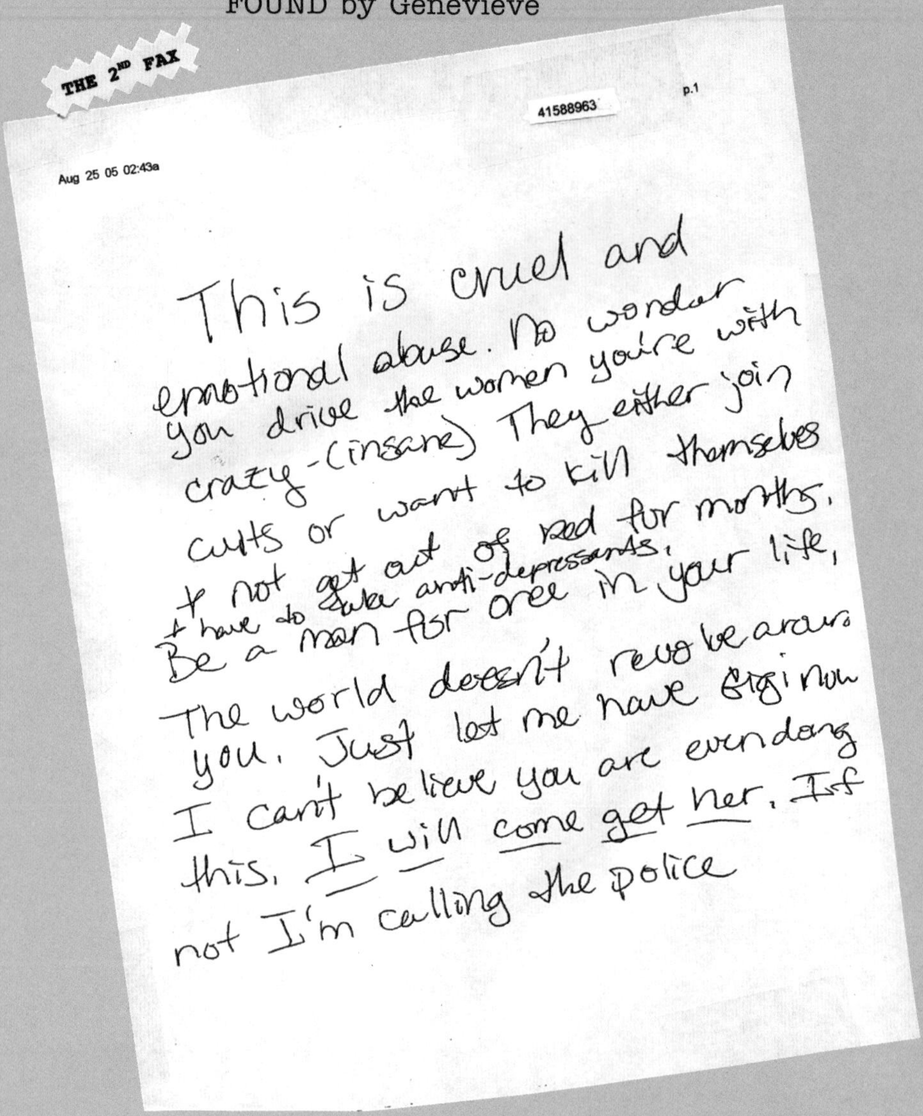

41588963   p.1

Aug 25 05 02:43a

This is cruel and emotional abuse. No wonder you drive the women you're with crazy—(insane) They either join cults or want to kill themselves + not get out of bed for months. + have to take anti-depressants. Be a man for once in your life, The world doesn't revolve around you. Just let me have Gigi now I can't believe you are even doing this, I will come get her. If not I'm calling the police

"These three faxes rolled off of our office fax machine in the middle of the night. Who's Gigi? A dog, cat, a child? Why is Gigi being held captive? I love the last page – oops – my bad!" **Genevieve**

12

41588963 p.1

Aug 25 05 02:36a

I just want
Gigi back! Tell me
where she is and I'll
come get her!
Why are you doing this??
Be a man!

Aug 25 05 02:56a

41588963 p.1

Sorry

wrong

number!

13

Steve

Steve Steve Steve Steve Steve

"This was on the floor of the laundry room in my apartment building. More baffling than the flyer itself is the fact that five people ripped off names."
Seth

14

MAKE DAMN SURE
FOUND by Dan Kallman

WARNING

The iguana is loose on the porch- Before entering, make damn sure that she is not going to bolt out the door when you open it; Also, be sure to close screen door til it latches shut!!!!
Thank you

OPEN AT 3
FOUND by Chris at Monkfish Books

"Two excuses are always better than one!" **Davy**

TODAY IS MY GRANDMOTHERS 100 BIRTHDAY
AND
THERE IS A RACOON IN MY BATHROOM. WILL OPEN AT 3AM
Thanks

15

"We love, because He first loved us." 1 John 4:19

I CARE...

About _My square head_

Who lives at _Circleville_

Because _I have a Big Square head_

_____

....and I want my church to help me put concern into action.

++++++++++++++++++++++++++

I WISH...

We would sing _give me a circle head_

The Pastor would preach a sermon

on _different people with different heads_

Someone would visit _the Square_

headed dude

Name ☐ head

Date _Who cares_

I/We communed ✗

I would like to.......

get a normal head

_____

_____

MY OWN PRIVATE LIBRARY
FOUND by Bill van Sickle

Thank you for the One-Cent #12!
Let us know what you are thinking. . .

Family, travel, community, literacy, spirit, dreams, business, future, puppies, hope, careers, hobbies, music, goals, news, recipes, fantasy, genealogy, tigers, employment and more!

Today in the library, I wanted to find _life, and it more abundantly..._

When I listen to music, I prefer _to be able to hear._

I want to learn more about the following topics or subjects _the Wombats' mating habits._

It would be easier to use the library if _you moved it directly to my house._

I wish my library had more _free money to give away._

☑ Yes, please share my comments with other library patrons!
Name (optional): _____

☐ No, please hold my comments in confidence.

Natrona County Public Library
(307) 237-4935 • http://library.natrona.net/

PLEASE DIE ALICIA

FOUND by Ruth Fertig

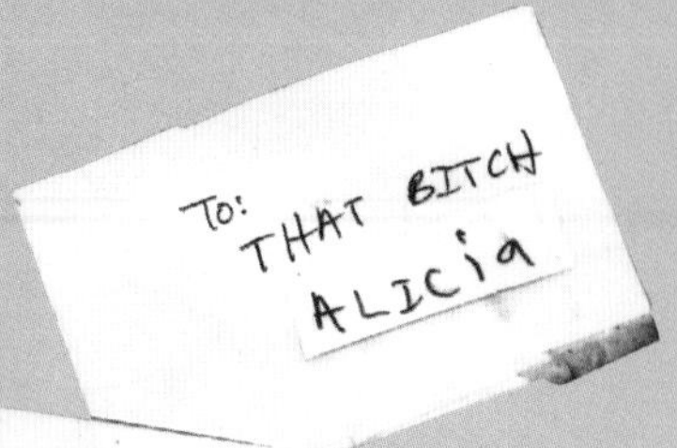

To:
THAT BITCH
ALICIA

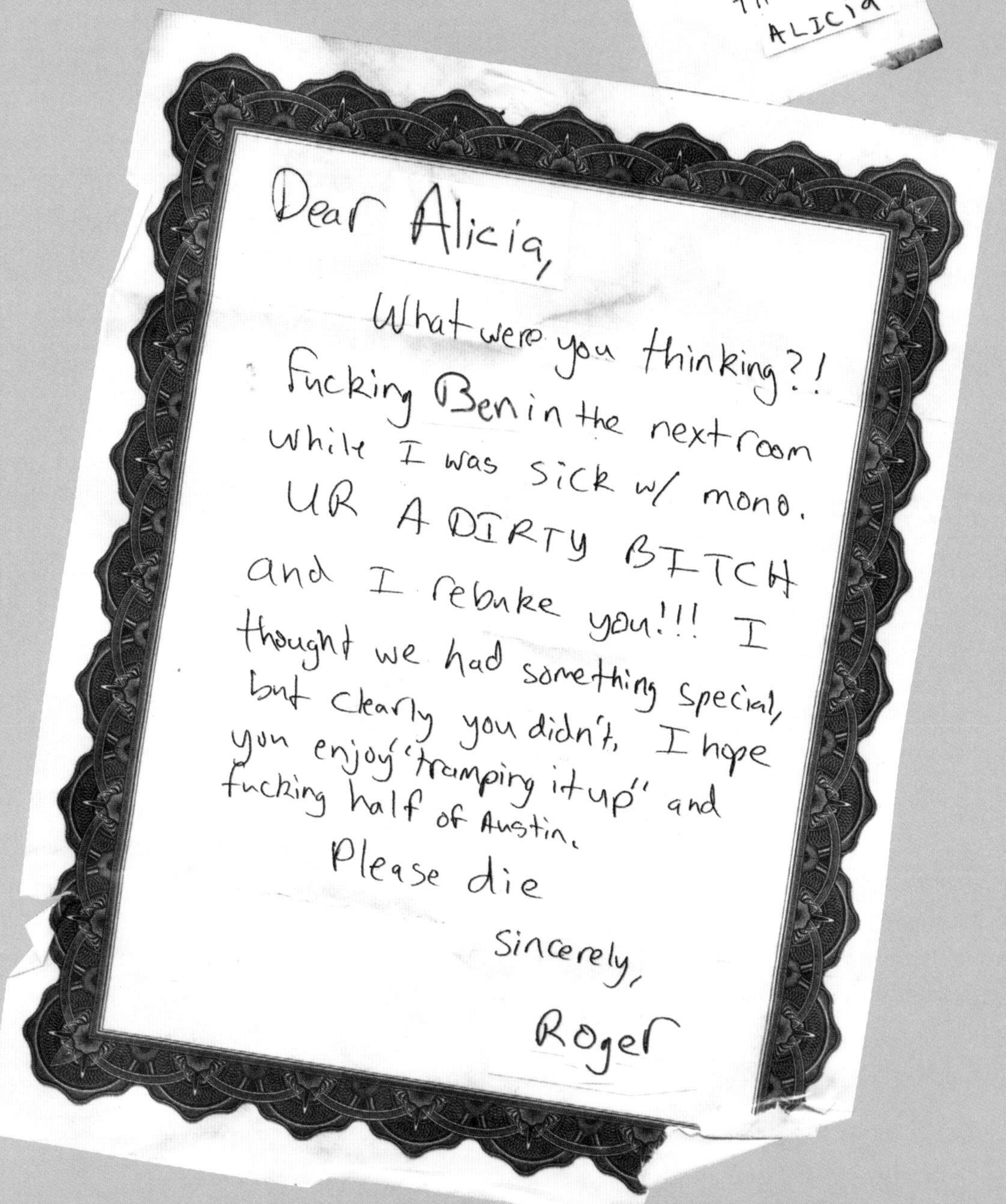

Dear Alicia,

What were you thinking?! fucking Ben in the next room while I was sick w/ mono. UR A DIRTY BITCH and I rebuke you!!! I thought we had something special, but clearly you didn't. I hope you enjoy "tramping it up" and fucking half of Austin.

Please die

Sincerely,

Roger

OLD POSTCARD
FOUND by Kevin Sampsell

OLD POSTCARD
FOUND by Cynthia Piper

"I found this postcard inside the wall of a demolished barn. The 90-year-old woman who lived there didn't remember this suitor, though she had three other sisters."
Cynthia

My Pretty Little Miss: — I must write you thus because I havent yet found out what your name is but I know where you live for I followed you home last night.

Say — if you are married tear this note up and dont tell your husband. If you are single and long for a life partner I am ready to leap without looking so long as I will find you where I land. If you want to meet me carry a newspaper under your arm tomorrow. I'll arrange it. — Expectantly.

© 1926 by Rr. Sup. Co., Chgo.

Hello. This note is going to seem very strange, and I have serious reservations about even writing it, but the circumstances are unusual, so I'll take a chance. I was on a walk tonight and I noticed that your car has Colorado plates. I met a girl several weeks ago (maybe 3), who was from Colorado, but I haven't run into her since. By chance, are you Julie who went to Creighton and is a pre-vet student @ the University? If so, I nervously introduced myself to you in the computer lab on the last day of summer session. You seemed like a very down to earth person and I hoped that we might meet again. I completely chickened out instead of giving you my phone number or asking you out, so I'm going out on a limb here by leaving a note. Trust me when I say that this is ⊕extremely⊕ out of character for me. I hope I haven't made you uncomfortable in anyway. You made an impression on me and I'd kick myself for not passing up a second opportunity to give you my #. Please don't take this as some kind of a crazy stalker note. Maybe I'll hear from you, though I'd be very surprised given how weird this seems. Take care.

— Alex 486-7579

P.S. If you're not Julie, then you should send this to Found magazine ~~~~ b/c it will be accepted!

"While I was busy getting drunk in celebration of landing a new job, young Alex was busy wondering if my Denver-based Volvo belonged to the one who got away. On July 14 I found this note attached to the front windshield of my car. Alex seems pretty sure you guys will like it, so I'm passing it on." **Charla**

DUDE, YOU BLEW IT
FOUND by Chris Willis

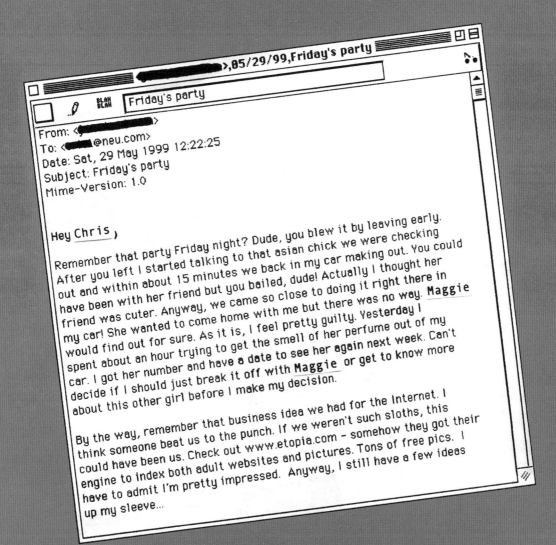

>,05/29/99,Friday's party

Friday's party

From: <▮▮▮▮▮▮▮▮▮▮▮>
To: <▮▮▮▮@neu.com>
Date: Sat, 29 May 1999 12:22:25
Subject: Friday's party
Mime-Version: 1.0

Hey Chris)

Remember that party Friday night? Dude, you blew it by leaving early. After you left I started talking to that asian chick we were checking out and within about 15 minutes we back in my car making out. You could have been with her friend but you bailed, dude! Actually I thought her friend was cuter. Anyway, we came so close to doing it right there in my car! She wanted to come home with me but there was no way. Maggie would find out for sure. As it is, I feel pretty guilty. Yesterday I spent about an hour trying to get the smell of her perfume out of my car. I got her number and have a date to see her again next week. Can't decide if I should just break it off with Maggie or get to know more about this other girl before I make my decision.

By the way, remember that business idea we had for the Internet. I think someone beat us to the punch. If we weren't such sloths, this could have been us. Check out www.etopia.com - somehow they got their engine to index both adult websites and pictures. Tons of free pics. I have to admit I'm pretty impressed. Anyway, I still have a few ideas up my sleeve...

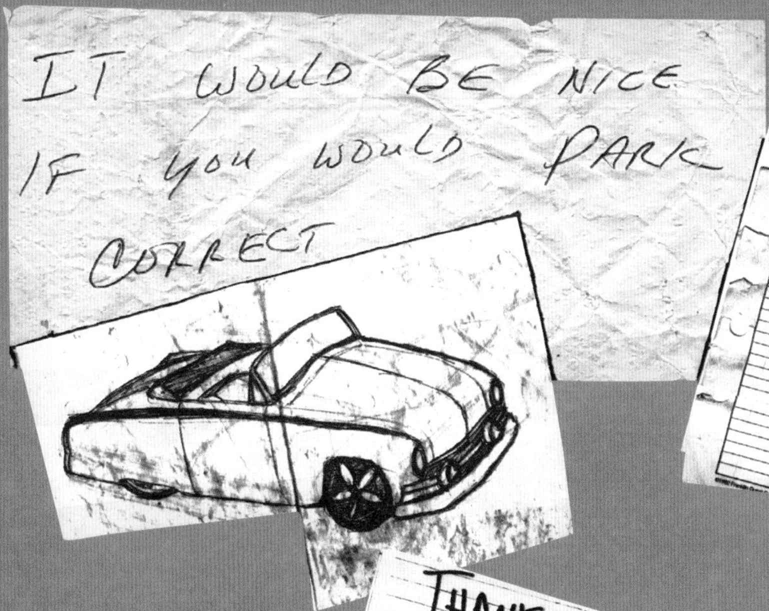

IT WOULD BE NICE IF YOU WOULD PARK CORRECT

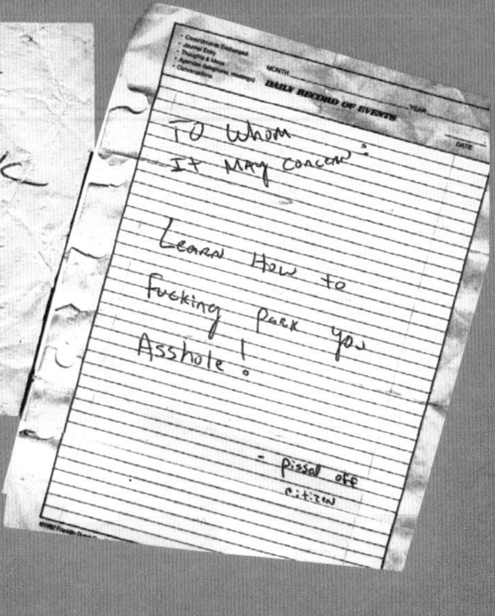

To Whom It May Concern

Learn How to Fucking Park you Asshole!

— Pissed off Citizen

BAD
WHY WOULD YOU PARK LIKE THIS?
TAKING UP TWO SPACES!

GOOD
TAKING UP ONLY ONE SPACE

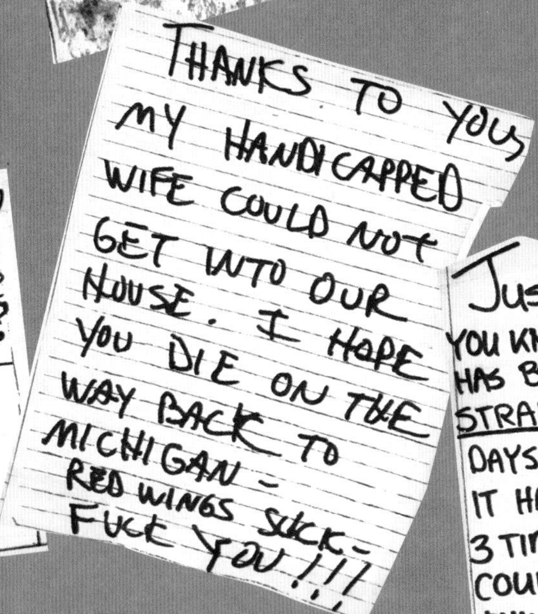

THANKS TO YOU, MY HANDICAPPED WIFE COULD NOT GET INTO OUR HOUSE. I HOPE YOU DIE ON THE WAY BACK TO MICHIGAN — RED WINGS SUCK — FUCK YOU!!!

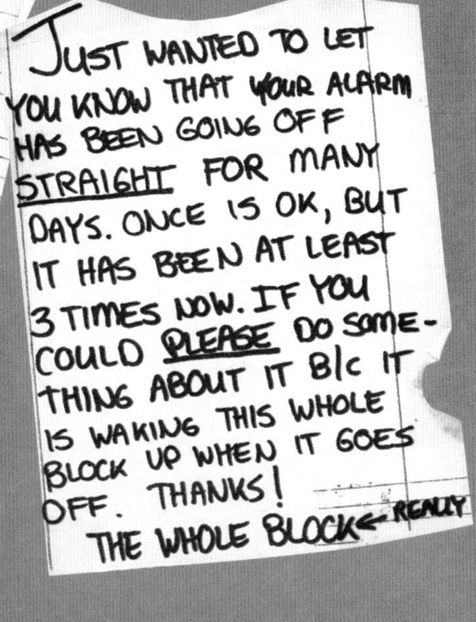

JUST WANTED TO LET YOU KNOW THAT YOUR ALARM HAS BEEN GOING OFF STRAIGHT FOR MANY DAYS. ONCE IS OK, BUT IT HAS BEEN AT LEAST 3 TIMES NOW. IF YOU COULD PLEASE DO SOME-THING ABOUT IT B/c IT IS WAKING THIS WHOLE BLOCK UP WHEN IT GOES OFF. THANKS!
THE WHOLE BLOCK ← REALLY

PARKING TICKETS

"So many delightfully rich parking notes have been FOUND and sent in..." **Davy**

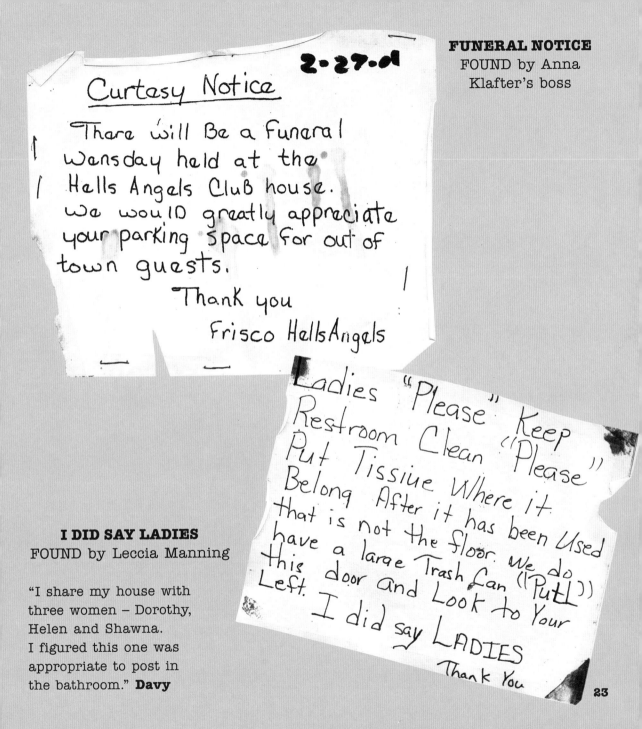

2-27-d

Curtesy Notice

There will Be a funeral Wensday held at the Hells Angels CluB house. We would greatly appreciate your parking space for out of town guests.
                    Thank you
                    Frisco HellsAngels

FUNERAL NOTICE
FOUND by Anna
Klafter's boss

I DID SAY LADIES
FOUND by Leccia Manning

"I share my house with three women – Dorothy, Helen and Shawna. I figured this one was appropriate to post in the bathroom." **Davy**

Ladies "Please" Keep Restroom Clean "Please" Put Tissiue Where it Belong After it has been Used that is not the floor. We do have a large Trash Can ((Put)) this door and Look to Your Left. I did say LADIES
                    Thank You

AJ,

We have your binder. You will never see it again unless you leave a sum of $3.50 directly under the clock to the left of the door at precisely 1:15. Please do not inform any teacher of this transaction. If you mess this up you WILL regret it.

If you do not comply than you will never see it again.

AJ,
we have
Your
binder!

← NO RETURN ADDRESS

Milwaukee, WI

FOUND Magazine
3455 Charing Cross Rd.
Ann Arbor, MI 48108-1911

48108*1911

BLACKMAIL
FOUND by Jennifer Jones

GRANDPA

FOUND by Damon Smith

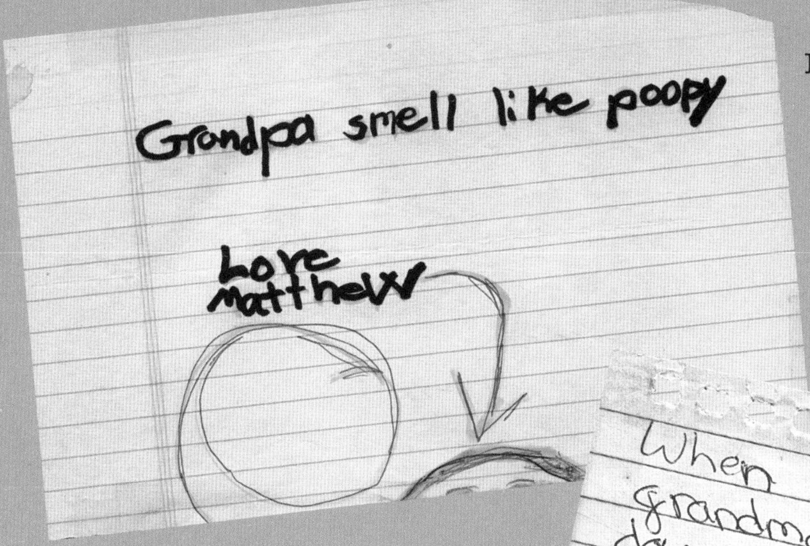

Grandpa smell like poopy

Love matthew

“Begs the questions:

1. Who was Matthew’s message of “love” given to?
2. What is the content of the detatched drawing?”

Damon

OTHER GRANDMAS

FOUND by David Lewis

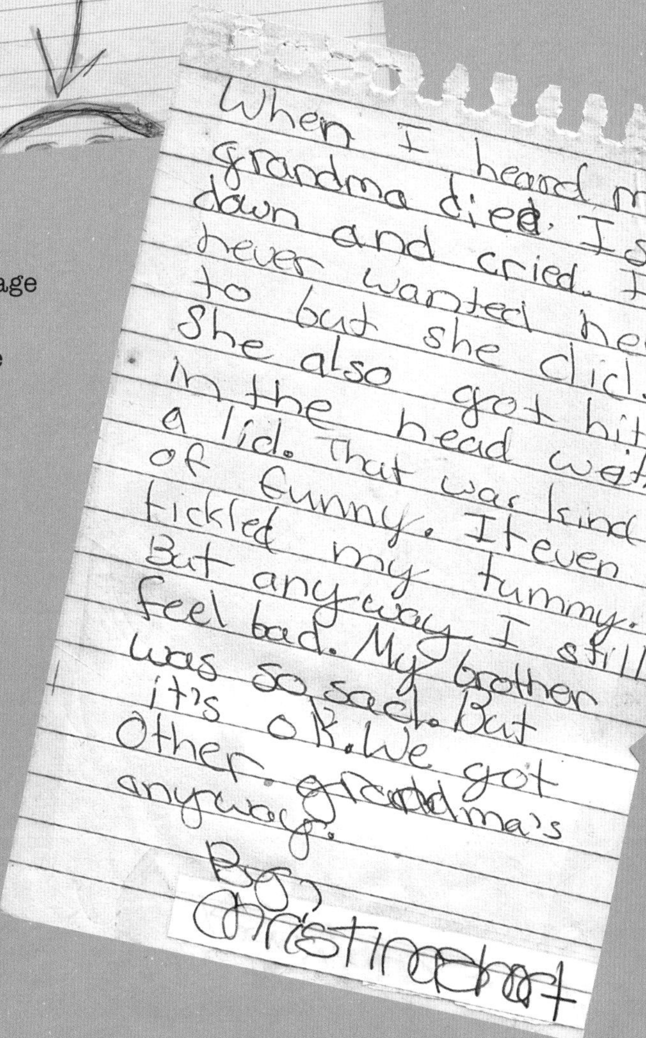

When I heard my grandma died, I sat down and cried. I never wanted her to but she did. She also got hit in the head with a lid. That was kind of funny. It even tickled my tummy. But anyway I still feel bad. My brother was so sad. But it's o.k. We got other grandma's anyway.

Bye,
Christine Hart

I, Al Burian, being of reasonably sound mind and body, do hereby deliver my last will and testament, on this morning of November 3, 2001. Should I die under circumstances other than the total collapse of civilization, i.e, if it's at all possible to arrange a funeral, I would like it to happen in the following manner: I'd prefer to be cremated, then have my remains laid into the earth in a ceremony where "Another one bites the dust" by Queen plays over a public address system. That should put people in a jovial mood and hopefully a good party will follow.

Signed,

AL BURIAN

witness ___Liz Saidel___

I, AL BURIAN...
FOUND by Dave Hopper

DEAR VANESSA
FOUND by Andy Freeburg

"Was this turned in as a paper for class? Looks like the teacher failed to see the humor." **Andy**

Unacceptable 0

2 f Ei   Street
Rap , East Carolina
November 30, 1093

Dear Vanessa

It's been a long hall for both of us. I found it hard to get used of being away from you. It went from having premarrital sex and then going to college and having sex with many women. I am writing you to tell that I miss having your small sexy ass, and pelvis depressing against the hair on my pelvis region. I missed having your glasses falling off because of the pain.

I thought to make things different this time we will have sex in front of your parents to see what their reaction will be. If they like it I will go after some of your sisters as well. If the relationship doesn't work out we can still have fun on the weekends

Seminal Vessicle,

Bryan Howard

INTERMARRIAGE
FOUND by Peter Rothbart

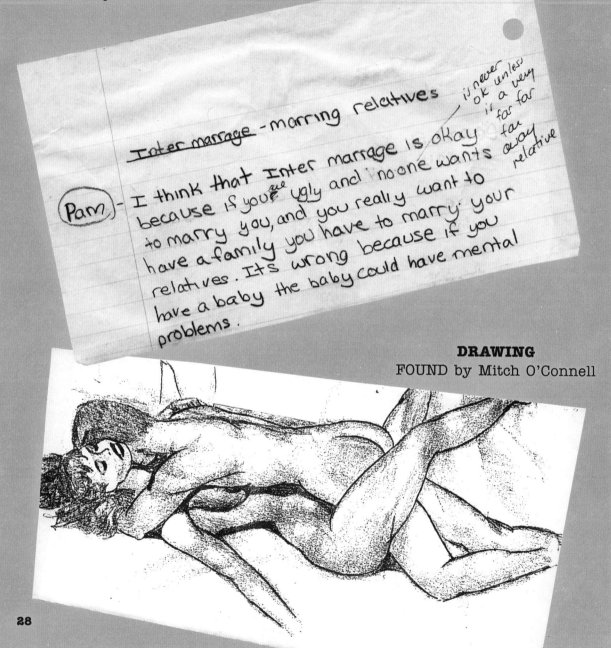

Inter marrage - marring relatives

is never ok unless it's a very far far away relative

Pam - I think that Inter marrage is okay because if your ugly and no one wants to marry you, and you really want to have a family you have to marry your relatives. It's wrong because if you have a baby the baby could have mental problems.

DRAWING
FOUND by Mitch O'Connell

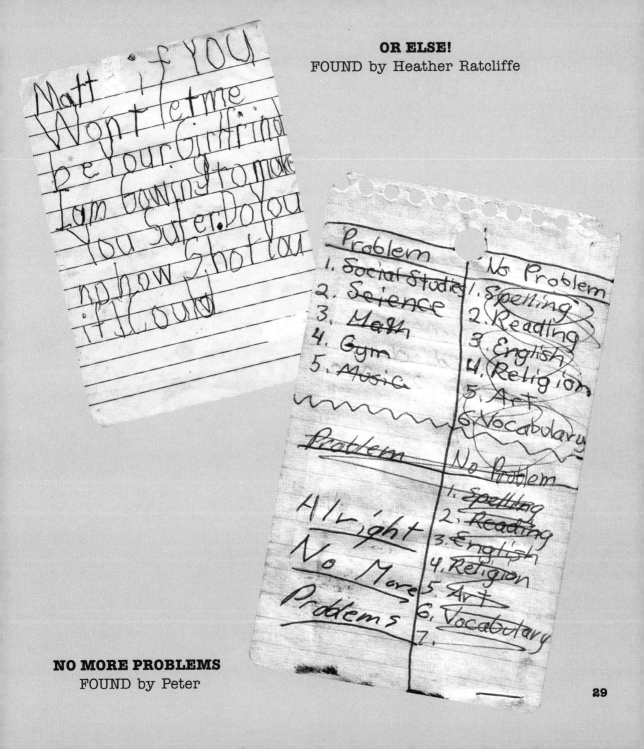

Matt if YOU
Won't let me
be Your GirlFriend
I am Going to make
You SuFer Do You
no how 2 hot cou
iF I could

Problem
1. Social Studies
2. Science
3. Math
4. Gym
5. Music

No Problem
1. Spelling
2. Reading
3. English
4. Religion
5. Art
6. Vocabulary

Problem

No Problem
1. Spelling
2. Reading
3. English
4. Religion
5. Art
6. Vocabulary
7.

Allright
No More
Problems

NO MORE PROBLEMS
FOUND by Peter

Bad things

Andrew | Paul
crazy | crazier
has issues w/ fat people | too loud
torn between Stacy & I | too childish

Good things

Andrew | Paul
married him | child
always been good friend | house
sex (?) | money

ANDREW VS PAUL
FOUND by Ivy Tominack

TIME OF THE ATTACK
FOUND by Matt Samford and Jason Affolder

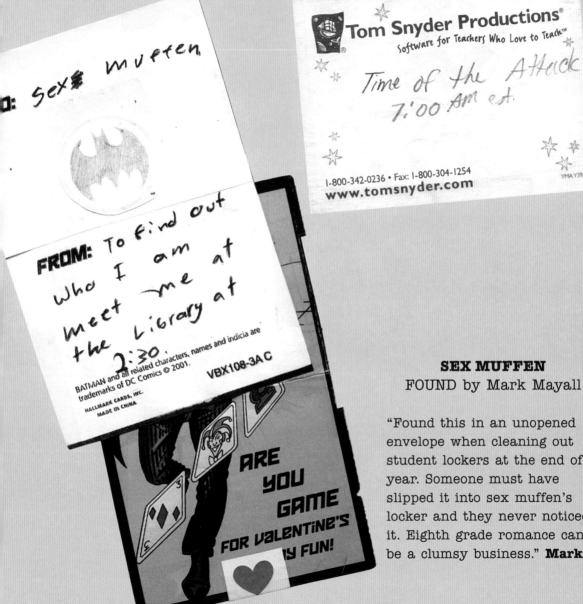

Tom Snyder Productions®
Software for Teachers Who Love to Teach™

Time of the Attack
7:00 AM est.

1-800-342-0236 • Fax: 1-800-304-1254
www.tomsnyder.com

YMAY398

□: Sex muffen.

FROM: To find out who I am
meet me at the Library at
2:30.

BATMAN and all related characters, names and indicia are
trademarks of DC Comics © 2001.

VBX108-3A C

HALLMARK CARDS, INC.
MADE IN CHINA

ARE YOU GAME FOR VALENTINE'S
Y FUN!

SEX MUFFEN
FOUND by Mark Mayall

"Found this in an unopened
envelope when cleaning out
student lockers at the end of
year. Someone must have
slipped it into sex muffen's
locker and they never noticed
it. Eighth grade romance can
be a clumsy business." **Mark**

RENT $450.00 $225.00 ON the 1st.
                 AND
                $225.00 ON the 15th

A PERSON I NEED

A Mother Type PERSON NOT to
OLD AND NOT to young.

A Mother type PERSON that is going
to be a Careprovide.

A Mother Type PERSON that can
give a Shot to ANY one.

A Mother Type PERSON that can
go to DANcings with me and go
Other PLACES with me.

A Mother Type PERSON that will
Stay with me for as long as I
NEED you.

A Mother type PERSON that will
help out with RENT AND
ELECTRicity.

A Mother Type PERSON that will
go to Church with me AND
hang out With me AND my
friends.

A Mother Type PERSON that will
Not leave me.

                        OVER

A Mother Type PERSON that Love's
ANY type of ANIMALS.

A Mother Type PERSON that is
Single and is going to Stay Single.

A Mother TYPE PERSON Here with me
Just in case of a fire or Accident.

A Mother type PERSON Here with me
Just in case Someone BREAKS in.

SomEone who is not too Load
AND Not have too MANY friends over.

SomEone who DOES Not SMOKE or
DRINK (or who will Smoke outside).

SomEone who will go GRocery Shopping
with me with me.

A Mother type PERSON that I
can talk to ANY time in the
Day or night.

A Mother type PERSON that has a
good AND funny Sense of Humor.

A Mother type PERSON that has
a Car.

A Mother type PERSON that will be
a very, very good friend to me.
                        OVER

A Mother Type PERSON that will
Not get upset at me for any thing.

A Mother Type PERSON that is Not
going to be to fussy about things.

A Mother Type PERSON that I CAN
trust.

A Mother Type PERSON That will
be understanding about every thing.

A Mother Type PERSON that can
teach me things I don't know.

A Mother type PERSON who is clean
AND Not messing.

If this is you CALL

ME At 503-4

ROOM FOR RENT
FOUND by Geoff Greene

32

SUGAR DADY
FOUND by Harry Brown

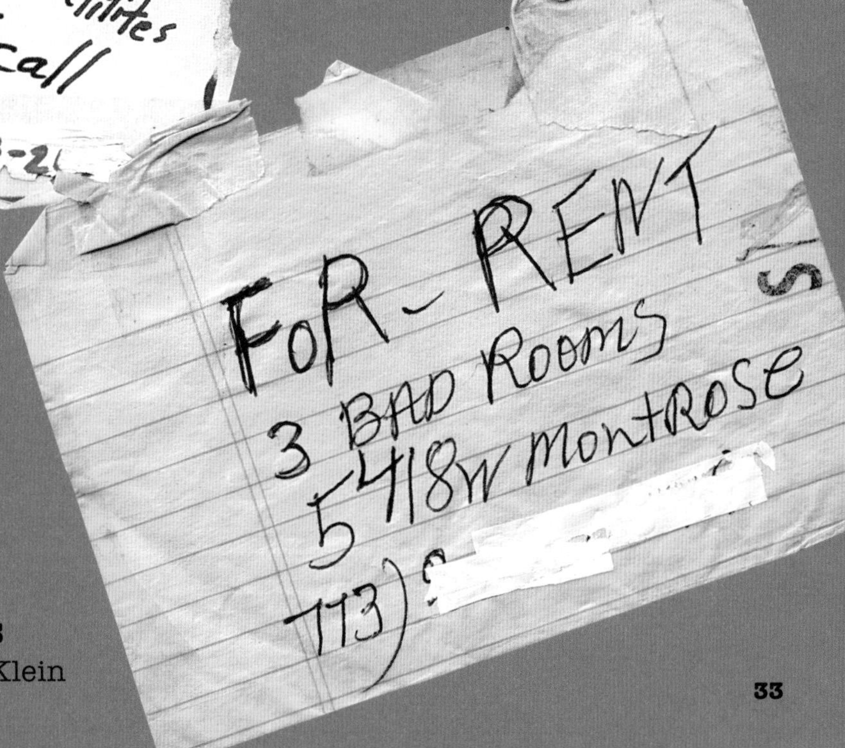

SUgar Dady

Looking For Roommit
Luissianna and TRumbll
Free For Femile
Free Rent and utilites
For More INF call
Sugar Dady At 713-2...

FOR - RENT
3 BAD Rooms
5 418W MontRose
773)

3 BAD ROOMS
FOUND by Brian Klein

Dear Santa,

This year I am going to try to be naughty and save you the trip. If not I will have a list at the ready. And I don't think your fat. I've watched Austin Powers. Should I give you cheese next year? Cause that girl in the commercial did and she got a car. A really nice car. I can't drive yet but oh well. Thank you for everything that you have given to me over the past years. You must be loaded. Can I have a slice of your mula? Thanks. Your Friend,
Howie Goetz

"From a whole folder of letters to Santa Claus behind an old desk in my office." **Megan**

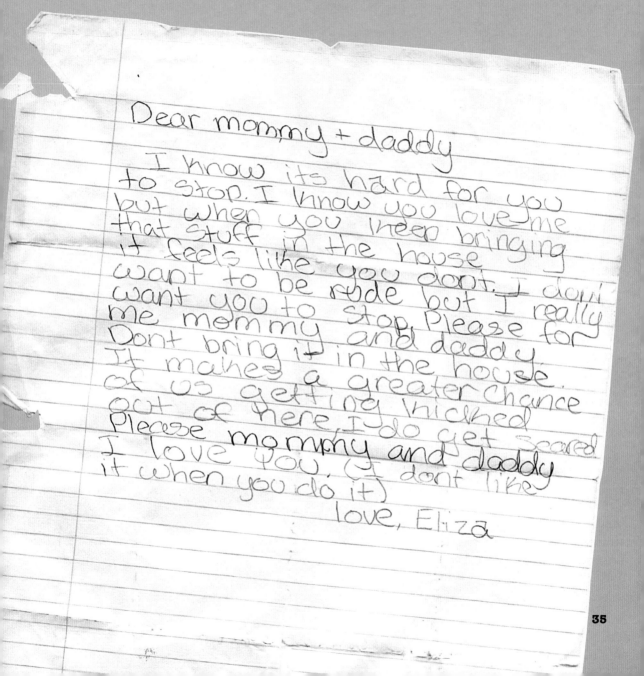

Dear mommy + daddy

I know its hard for you to stop. I know you love me but when you keep bringing that stuff in the house it feels like you dont. I dont want to be rude but I really want you to stop. Please for me mommy and daddy. Dont bring it in the house. It makes a greater chance of us getting kicked out of here. I do get scared Please mommy and daddy I love you. (I dont like it when you do it)

love, Eliza

After leaving the building, please...

LOCK THIS DOOR

It will prevent unauthorized people from entering the building and **defecating** *in the washing machine. Many thanks!*

"Note that those who are authorized to defecate in the washing machine will be given a key for entry!" **Popcorn Pete**

To cashier:
Will you please sell my son one pack of Newport Lights.

Thank you for your help

If I Go 2 get A beer
I'll miss the bus home,
I'll have to walk. oh, A Longwalk
if I get the bus I won't
have time 2 get a beer.
no beer after 2:00, no beer...
bus or beer
bus or beer...
I walk, I walk
I walk with beer
close 2 my heart I
hold her, she has not been
opened yet. I walk-
could it be? yes! yes!
THE BUS! Ive never been
so happy for a bus 2. B Late!

BUS OR BEER
FOUND by Steve Heiug

AARON'S ALGEBRA TEST
FOUND by David Meiklejohn

Determine if the example models exponential growth or exponential decay. Then find the percent increase or decrease.

① $y = 620(.94)^x$

② $y = 54(1.07)^x$

Graph each function.

③ $y = 5.3(.4)^x$

x	y
0	4
1	3
2	2
3	1
4	0

④ $y = 3(2)^x$

x	y
8	9
6	10
420	50
69	75

⑤ You put $2,000 into an account earning 4% interest compounded continuously. Find the amount at the end of 8 years.

Not enough

⑥ Write an equation to describe each exponential function $y = ab^x$. The base is 8 and the graph passes through the point (4,3).

X-Q = ABCDEFGHI JKLMNOPQR
         TUVWXYZ

Evaluate each expression by first rewriting it as an exponential equation.

⑦ $Log_2 16$

Logggg/6

⑧ $Log_5 125$

Logggg/25

⑨ $Log_4 \frac{1}{64}$

Logggg 16

Expand the following.

⑩ $Log\ 3x^2$

$Log\ 6 \times 12$

⑪ $Log\ \frac{4y}{x^3}$

Condense the following.

⑫ $Log\ 7 + 2\ Log\ A - 5\ Log\ B$

It's small enough

⑬ Expand $Log_3\ 14$ into an expression with two logarithmic terms.

$150 ÷ 2 = 75 \times 2 = 150 ÷ 2 = 75 \times 2 = 150 ÷ 2 = 75 \times 2 = 150 ÷ 2 =$ Correct answer

⑭ Use the properties of logarithms to evaluate $Log\ 5 + Log\ 10 + Log\ 2$.

Get off my Property !!!!

— DAVY

the following Equations.

$x^4 = 81$

Yahoo
Yahoo
Yahoo
Yahoo

$x^{\frac{3}{2}} - 5 = 59$

⑯ $Log\ 5x = 3$

Yahoo
Yahoo
Yahoo
Yahoo
Yahoo

⑰ $10^{2x} = 40$

Yahoo
Yahoo
Yahoo
Yahoo

⑲ $4e^{2x} = 14$

⑳ $Ln(2x+5) = 10$

My name is Aaron
I'm in Algebra Two
I sit in class for an hour
And nothing I do

What Killian is talking about
I guess I'll never know
But its stuff I should've learned
A long time ago

But I just sat in his room
watching the time pass
And all I would do
Is sit on my as—

My hopes of passing
Is no hope at all
I just stare at the board
And watch my grade fall

Maybe someday
My grade will go higher
But who am I kidding
I'm only a lyer.

This Algebra year
In June will soon stop
And that means my grade
Can no longer drop

YAY!!!

Me

You

"This has become one of my favourite finds of all-time. It's clear Aaron is having his struggles with algebra, but I love what he's done here. Aaron's total score for this test, which includes a series of rhymed couplets on the back, is zero." **Davy**

39

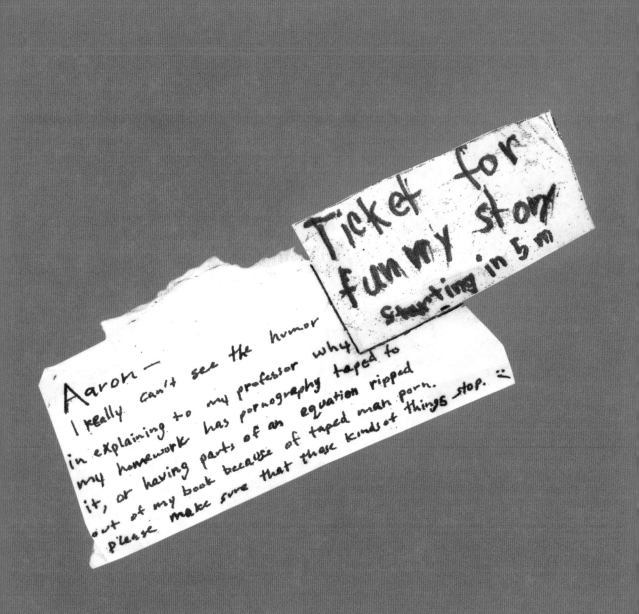

Aaron —
I really can't see the humor in explaining to my professor why my homework has pornography taped to it, or having parts of an equation ripped out of my book because of taped man porn. please make sure that these kinds of things stop. :⁻)

Ticket for funny story
Starting in 5 m

AARON, NO HUMOUR & STARTING IN 5 M
FOUND by by Susannah Felts, John Kovacs, Jordan Morris

PSYCHO
FOUND by Anne Gunnison

LOST COBRA

Color: brown, black, yellow, red (on teeth), blue (color of tongue)

Snake has been known to bite off heads.

Snake is not house trained.
ANSWERS TO "PSYCHO".
Length: 7'
Weight: 45 lbs

Warning, snake is deadly.
Will bite if provoked.

IF FOUND, CALL (510) 3:

Psycho has strong scottish accent

To the Person who stole my food from the small brown refrigerator (consisting of hummus, mango salsa, leaf lettuce, tortilla, and guacamole), please note that I ate from the containers. If you begin to experience flu-like symptoms, please see a medical doctor.

PLEASE SEE A MEDICAL DOCTOR
FOUND by Mrs M Pan

Jessie

I did not take anything. I know there's no convincing you once you've made up your mind. And although I cannot offer you any other explanation as to what happened to it. That doesn't mean I did it. How could I have? You say your car was locked and Katie had the keys?

Anyway, I don't need to take something of yours when I can get my own. I doesn't make sense.

So here is a replacement. Cuz I can't stand it when you think I've wronged you

— mom

Dear Delane,   October 21, 2003.
          You and I are just
friends. That's the way I
wish to remain. I like you
but only as a friend. I would
be happy If this doesn't
effect our bond — as friends.
     Please understand it is
not because your black.
   It's not because your not
handsome enough it's just
because you and I are
friends, And that's it.
     The reason you can't
be my boyfriend is because
I am not attract to you
as you are to me. To be
honest I just want
us to be friends that's
all.   It's your choice
whether you want to
be my friend or not.
                    Julia

JUST FRIENDS
FOUND by Jen Devoe

"I wonder if Delane ever got the subtle hint that she just
wanted to be friends." **Jen**

LAUGHS
FOUND by Crystal Brown

"My daily commute to work takes me through the backwoods of West Virginia. A couple of months ago I saw this sign in blue pain nailed to a tree by the side of the road."
Crystal

I HOPE YOU GOT YOUR LAUGHS

I will **Kill** you if you Touch!!

Dont make me do it, I dont like violence... but I will Kill you if I have To.

Thank you

P.J.

VIOLENCE
FOUND by Mike Montedoro Jr.

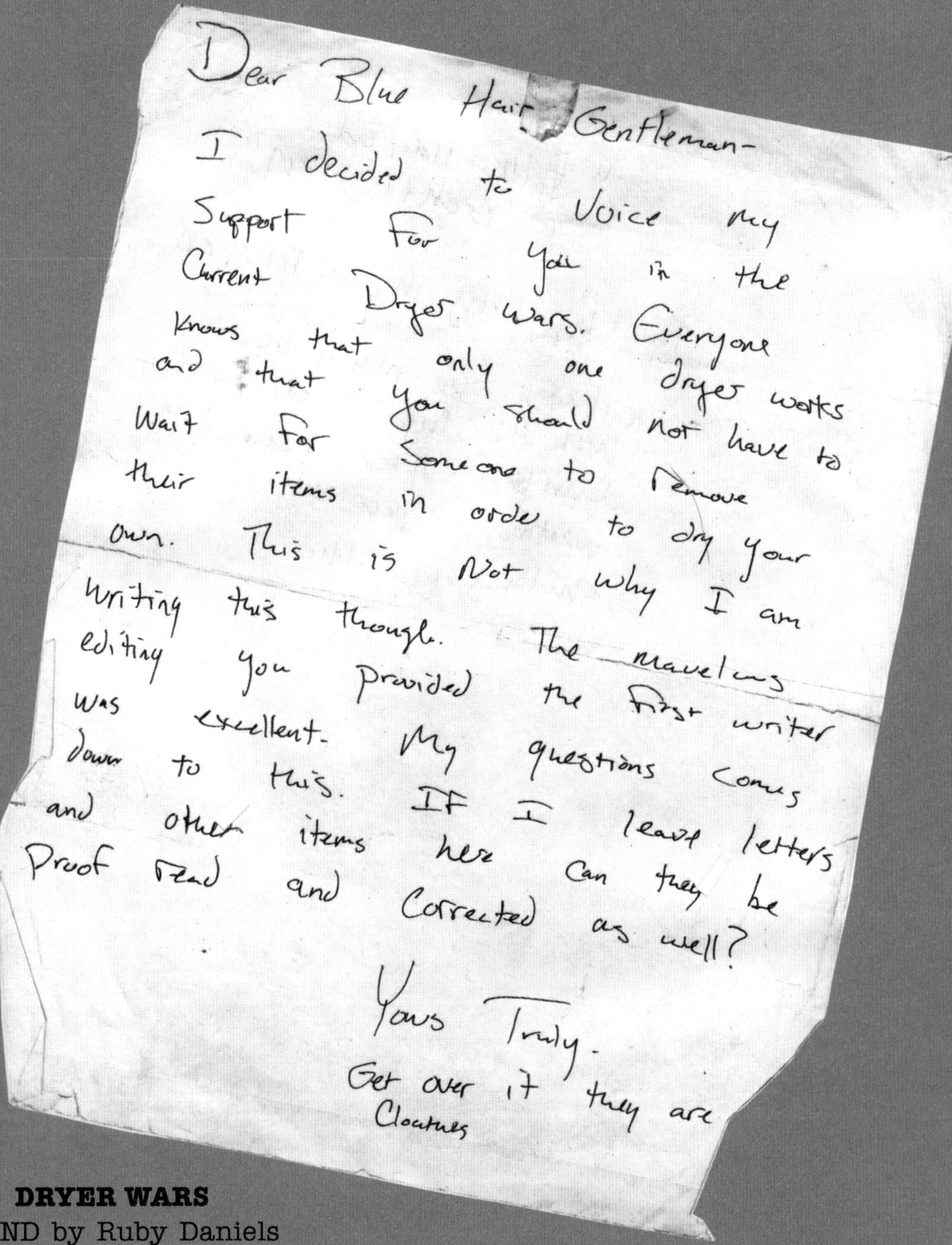

Dear Blue Hair Gentleman—

I decided to voice my support for you in the current Dryer Wars. Everyone knows that only one dryer works and that you should not have to wait for someone to remove their items in order to dry your own. This is not why I am writing this though. The marvelous editing you provided the first writer was excellent. My questions comes down to this. If I leave letters and other items here can they be proof read and corrected as well?

Yours Truly.

Get over it they are Cloathes

DRYER WARS
FOUND by Ruby Daniels

There is a person in our immediate area who is trapping our neigborhood cats and I have no idea where he is taking them. I am effected because between my across the street neighbor and myself, we have 5 ferile cats who are all spayed and neutered, and we feed them. Noone in the neighborhood objects to the cats except the person who is doing this terrible deed. I have received a letter of complaint from the city which I have responded to. Last week, I noticed one of the cats gone. I was afraid it might have been hit by a car, but there were no traces. The missing cat had only 1 eye, as I had to have an operation on him years ago, since the cat had such a bad infection, it was blind in that eye anyway. The cats are all from the same litter in 1998. At any rate within the last 2 days, another cat is not showing up for meals. Yesterday morning I was walking my dogs when suddenly I noticed this neighbor had an animal trap with cat food set in it. The trap was in his front yard mostly covered by bushes. I took pictures of the trap in front of his house. I confronted him with the disappearances today, and asked where he took the cats. He just said, "Did you see me take your cats. I don't know what you are talking about." I am so upset having raised these cats from kittens in the neighborhood, that I don't know what to do. I contacted the animal shelter and when they get around to it, they will send an officer to see if he has a permit, which I'm sure he doesn't. If everyone could write him imploring him not to do what he is doing, that may help. I am so afraid the officer might get there after all the cats are gone, and God only knows where he is taking them. I just found out that another neighbor is missing a cat. I am leaving his address in case someone can pass this on to anyone who can help. Thank you. The person who is trapping the cats is...

Frank Talbert
3663 Baytree Blvd.
San Luis Obispo, CA 92609
(805) 316-48

TRAPPING OUR CATS
FOUND by Dan Tice

6/25/2004 9:26 AM

Dear Neighbor:

It has come to my attention that my neighbor has sent out a memo throughout our community stating false information about me.

I can assure you that his accusations are absolutely not true. He has stated in his memo that I am trapping cats. This is not true. I have not - nor do I ever intend to trap cats.

I set out a humane rat / gopher trap which is what my neighbor saw on my property. The trap has always been empty in the three days that it was set. I did not catch gophers, rats or any other animals. I assured him that I am not targeting his cats or anyone else's cats. He was so irate that I have since thrown the humane trap away.

However, since the sending of my neighbor's anonymous letter giving out my address and phone number, I have received voicemail messages to my home threatening to poison and shoot my dog. I have turned over the recorded messages to the police department.

The purpose of this memo is to assure you, my neighbors, that I am not trapping cats. Please feel free to contact me if you have further questions or concerns.

Thank you,

Frank
(805) 316-48

"I found these notices among other papers and debris in the trunk of an old Chevy I bought in suburban LA." **Dan**

47

13 Things to do today

1. Pray to God for guidance
2. Find local cat for blood Sacrifice to ensure He is listening
3. Kick DOG for recent barking / find electro shock collar online
4. Beat girlfriend A (because she likes it)
5. FUCK girlfriend B (because she wants it)
6. Call and torment girlfriend C (because she needs it)!
7. Untie the neighbors ?
8. talk it over w/ them. MAYBE we can work it out w/out DEATH or the Police! ☺ Lets Hope!
9. Thaw out chicken in freezer
10. Call Nanny for recipe — Chicken Pot Pie & ??.....
11. I have it !! Apple Pie !! Yeah !! Alright !!
12. Buy an issue/copy of "The Collector" — All The great Killer's Killers have read it! Yeah! LEARN FROM THE BEST !!
13. Russian Roulete...BANG! BANG! HA! HA!

13 THINGS
FOUND by Dan Tice

48

MISSING

A

CHICKEN?

If you or anyone you know is
missing a chicken please call:

848-9669

Date:

10/11/98

REWARD
LOST CAT

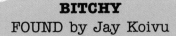

ANSWERS TO THE NAME
BITCHY
LAST SEEN AT THE CORNER OF
JUNE and DE LONGPRE
12/8/2002
IF FOUND, PLEASE CONTACT US AT:
323//

BITCHY
FOUND by Jay Koivu

PERFECTLY SAFE CAKE

FOUND by Kristina Hallez

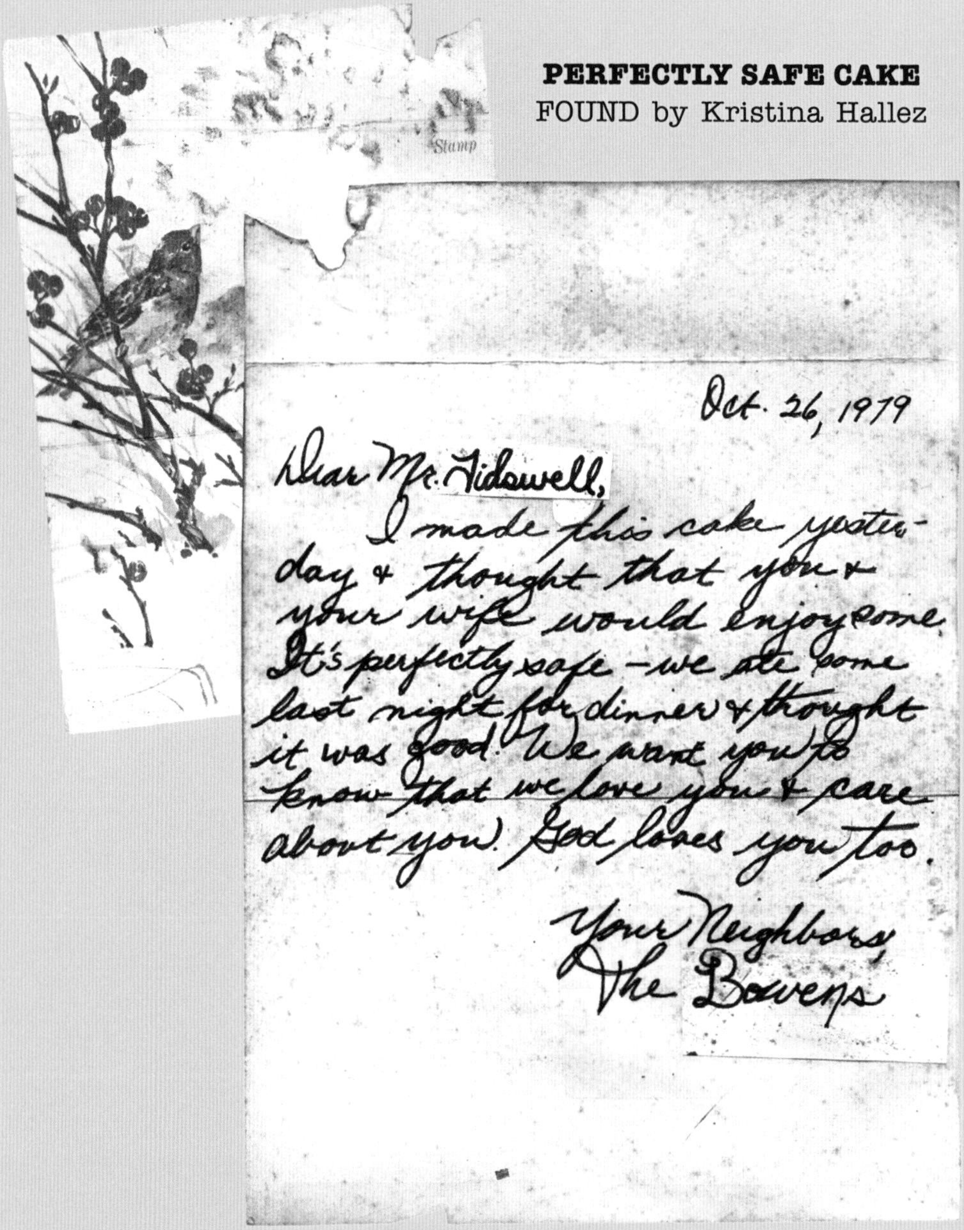

Oct. 26, 1979

Dear Mr. Tidswell,

I made this cake yesterday & thought that you & your wife would enjoy some. It's perfectly safe – we ate some last night for dinner & thought it was good. We want you to know that we love you & care about you. God loves you too.

Your Neighbors,
The Bowens

"This note seems like something a cartoon character would write after it had hidden a stick of dynamite in the cake."
Kristina

Feb 14, 200_

Dear Sean
Have a
great day!

Well Sean, hope you are losing some weight. Jan put a $100.00 in your bank account. It is from Gramma Jeannette for Valentine's day gift so you can afford diet & healthy food. fresh vegetables & apples instead of sugar stuff. I am worried about you gaining weight. You are too heavy. Time to stop it now. I hope Jan weighed you before you left on Monday!
Love You
Gramma Jeannette.
X O X O X O

CIRCLE YES/NO

FOUND by Harley Brown

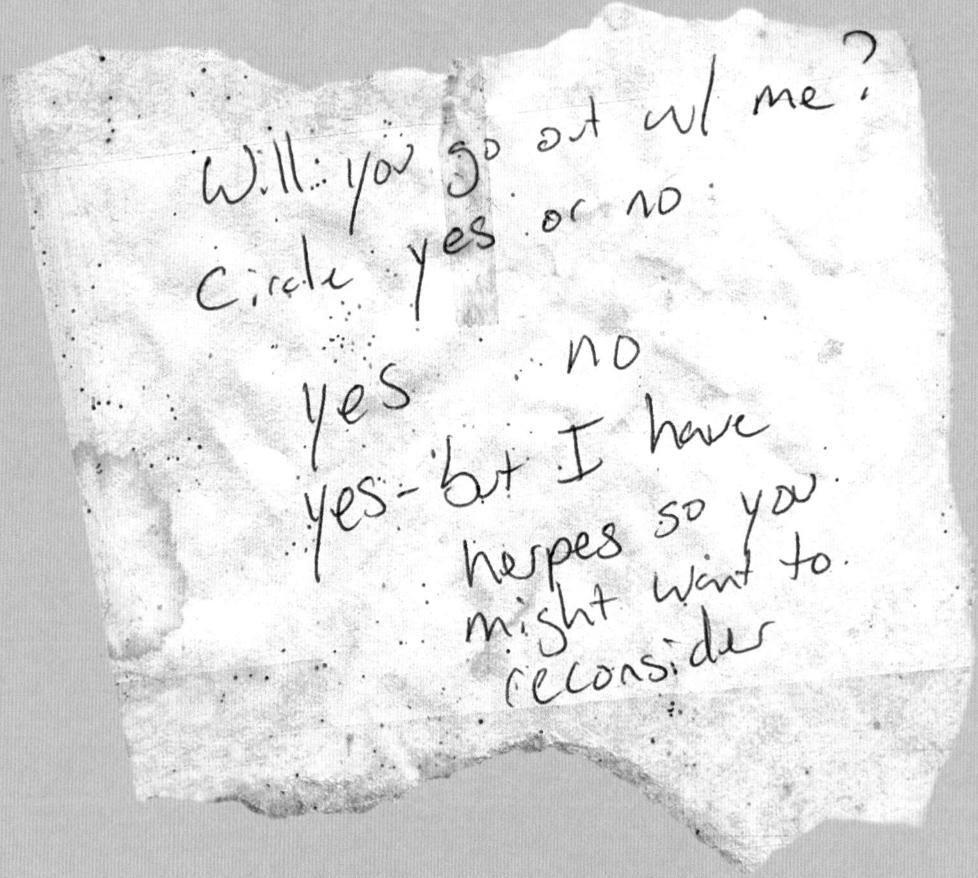
Will you go out w/ me?
Circle yes or no
yes no
yes - but I have
herpes so you
might want to
reconsider

The Condom made a mistake and broke.

You will never have sex ever agin

EVER AGAIN
FOUND by Meghan Jobson

"This note was on the street for a
week before I picked it up." **Jelly**

To whoever Finds
this I hope your
life is PERFECT or PERFECTO.
my father + step mom was
Killed while I was in the
house.
   My Grandma Aunt,
      Unkle All turned
their Back on me
my dream is to become
A Moolle someday I hope

Good luck to your
         your
         dreams.
STRANGER
   Monique

Radisson.
HOTELS WORLDWIDE
The difference is genuine. sm

54

Michigan Department of Corrections
PRISONER STATIONERY

TO:
NAME

NO. AND STREET OR R.R.

CITY

IN CORRESPONDENCE, USE NAME AND NUMBER ON YOUR LETTER AND ENVELOPE.

STATE | ZIP

FROM:
NAME

NO.

INSTITUTION | LOCK

DATE

4835-3110
CSJ-110

In 1979, I was residing in San Fransico. Given the pristen Ley beautiful weather, I opted To Traverse home on Foot one Evening a The sky was Arrestingly beautiful; The Night breeze carried the exotic fragrance of A cinnamon Tree. The crisp, Soothing Night Air served to remind me of other times-other place. I was Elated because I had Just got paid.

Suddenly, I reached the Golden Gate Bridge. I had the sublime feeling that something was Askew. upon closer inspection, I observed A MAN reading to Jump. I Approached with caution,
"What's the matter, Sir," I Asked. "I have No income, No Job, Life the desolete man exclaimed.

Being A small businessman, I offered him a job. That was 3 years ago. Now Bob works gainfully For me. Last week, I promoted him to Assistant manager.

I was glad that I opted To walk that Night.

The End

By: D. Argero

55

Sir Speedy®
PRINTING • COPYING • DIGITAL NETWORK

303-289-4747

8310 North Washington
Denver, CO 80229
Fax: 303-288-1874

Fitness Plan (:)

5-6 meals a day ← this is most important 2 - are shakes

NO STARBUC'S - saves $ & calories

NO DRINKING ~ wine (1 glass w/ meal :!)

5-10 warm up
30-50 lift
10-20 cool down w/ stretching

8-10 glasses H$_2$O - also important
SEX - LOTS of it!!

2002

FITNESS PLAN
FOUND by Alan Thompson

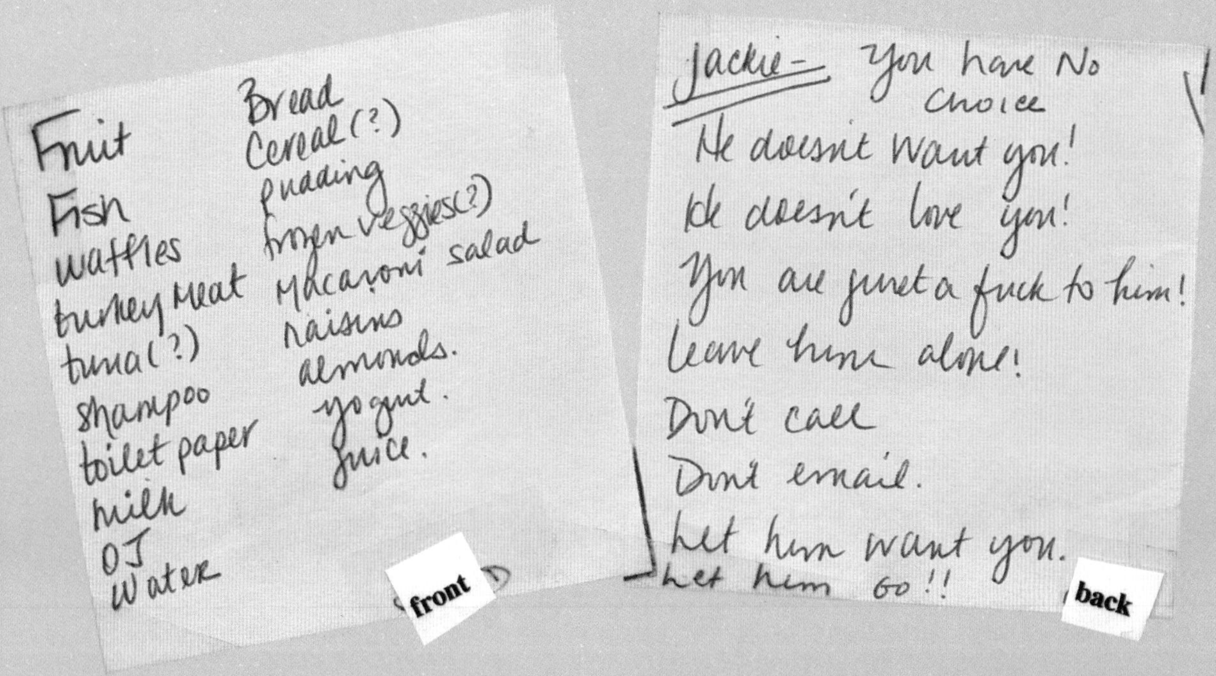

Fruit   Bread
Fish   Cereal (?)
Waffles   pudding
turkey Meat frozen veggies(?)
tuna(?) Macaroni salad
shampoo raisins
toilet paper almonds.
milk   yogurt.
OJ   Juice.
Water

front

Jackie— You have No Choice
He doesn't Want you!
He doesn't love you!
You are just a fuck to him!
Leave him alone!
Don't call
Don't email.
Let him want you.
Let him Go!!

back

NO CHOICE!

FOUND by Steven Lester

57

$5 FOR GAS
FOUND by Michelle Skinner

SMILE
FOUND by Wendy Fitzgerald

+Frank
I'll know longer call u by dad. I'd like & change my last name back and I hope my mother gets a divorce & u and I've never liked u.
                    —Rebecca

CRAB ON CAR
FOUND by Ed Faktorovitch

PLEASE DO NOT PUT CRAB ON MY CAR JUST CUT IT OUT ! ! !

DEAR BRO

FOUND by Shyan Silva

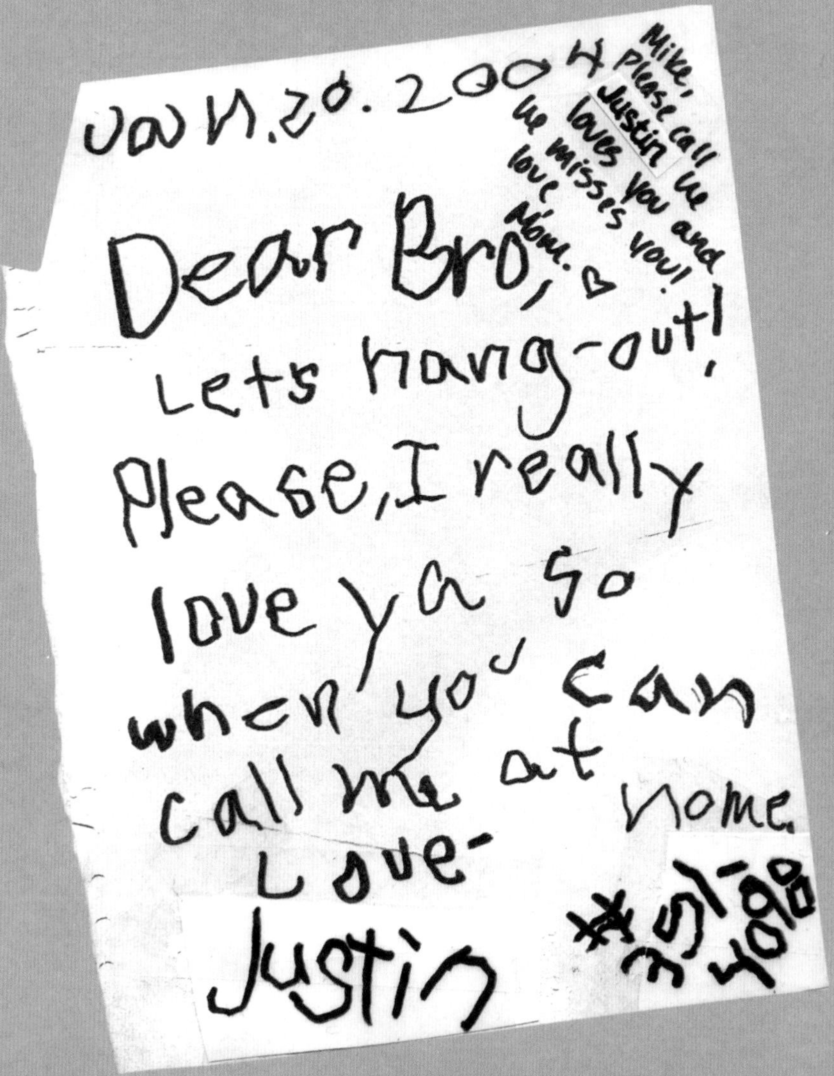

Jan. 20. 2004

Mike,
Please call
Justin he
loves you and
he misses you!
love,
Mom. ♥

Dear Bro,
Lets hang-out,
Please, I really
love ya so
when you can
call me at
home.
Love-
Justin
#351-4098

OUR SON:

WERE YOU OK IN THE PASSING OF THE YEAR? THE TIME GOES SO SWIFTLY, WE FELT IT'S A PITY THAT WE DIDN'T HAVE A CHANCE TO CELEBRATE YOUR BIRTH DAY. I DOUBT THAT WHETHER I CAN RECOGNIZE YOU WHEN I SEE YOU. **WE ARE GOING TO MOVE**, WE HOPE YOU COME HOME AND LIVE WITH US HAPPILY. PLEASE CONTACT WITH US AS SOON AS POSSIBLE. YOUR FAMILY'S TELEPHONE NUMBER : (416) 490-72... YOU CAN CALL US ANY TIME. WE ARE LOOKING FORWARD TO YOUR COMING HOME. HAVE A NICE DAY, OUR YOUNGEST BOY IN OUR FAMILY. WE LOVE YOU FOREVER.

YOUR FAMILY

SEPT, 10, 2005.

DEAR SON
FOUND by Jenn Lawrence

SWEET PACKET
FOUND by Ian Donahue.

"I found this at the Broad Ripple Brew pub mixed in with the other sugar packets." **Ian**

WEDDING BANDS FOR SALE
FOUND by Melissa Walker

TOMORROW
FOUND by Jessica Everson

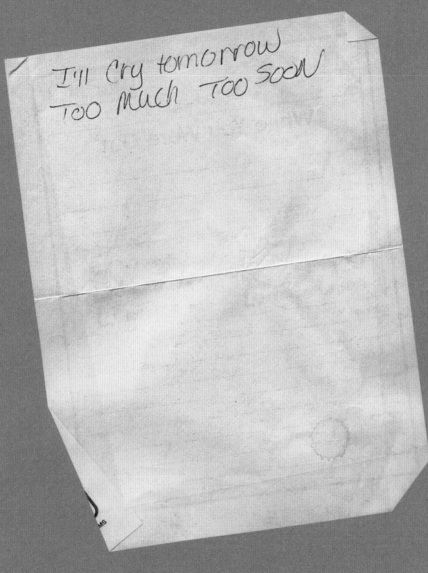

"I'm amazed at the power of these seven words." **Davy**

THANKS FOR EVERYTHING
FOUND by
Jordan Small and Nick

"I leave this one rumpled casually on the floor by the foot of my bed, so that anyone who's hanging out in my room will think I'm some kind of player." **Davy**

Thanks for everything! I had so much fun last night" ♥ Heather

HE'S IN SAN FRANSISCO
FOUND by Liam Gray

soy osama bin Laden, estoy en san francisco!

PORSCHE MEN
FOUND by Valerie Ferrier

date only men
with Porsche — (Rules)

Displaced southern Belle looking for
Heathcliff. Tired of wearing my
curtains. — ~~Financially secure~~ ~~and~~ ~~sexuality~~
~~appealing.~~
Understands Goethe's Couplets.
Knows Madame Butterfly isn't a stripper
in Vegas.

Secure enough to know what he
wants and to handle a woman who
~~does as well.~~
You can be a gentleman and understand
the qualities of partnership.

Recognizes at least some of the
following: Van Gough, Guttenberg, Arch'd Triumph,

ISN'T A STRIPPER
FOUND by Anna Belden and Jim McKay

HOTMAIL PROCRASTINATION
FOUND by Matt Summers

"I found this in a computer lab at one of Johns Hopkins University's D.C. campuses. This guy Sam seems interested in Lisa. I wonder if he made himself too available, though." **Matt**

Hotmail Home | Inbox | Compose | Contacts Options Help

accorrales@hotmail.com

Previous Next | Close

Save Address(es) Block

From : Sam   <   ...@hotmail.com>
Reply-To :   ...@alum.mit.edu
To :   ...@alum.swarthmore.edu
Subject : dinner, or lunch
Date : Mon, 08 Jul 2002 00:36:30 +0000

Printer Friendly Version

Reply Reply All Forward Delete Put in Folder...

Lisa

OK, I am going to procrastinate from cleaning the bathroom for a little longer by emailing you to follow up on my phone call....

First, congrats on getting your midterm behind you! Always good to get those out of the way!

Given your class schedule (I think you said always Tues and Thurs; sometimes Wed). For that reason, how about one of the following:

dinner on July 12, (Wed 17), 20, 21, 22, (Wed 24), 27, 28, 29, 30.
lunch on July 9, 11, 12, 17, 20, 21, 22, 24, 27, 28, 29, 30.

Let me know, and I hope you had a great time in Baltimore on the 4th!!!

Hoping to see you soon!
-Sam

Join the world's largest e-mail service with MSN Hotmail. http://www.hotmail.com

Previous Next | Close

Reply Reply All Forward Delete Put In Folder...

"Part of me wonders if the professor might have been appreciative of the brutal honesty and hilarity of the translation." **Kate**

Sent
Friday, November 19, 2004 2:32 pm
To
  how.howell oberlin.edu
Subject
memo

professor Howell,

Sorry for the late notice but I am having a very difficult time getting my memo done. I was absent from class on wenesday as well as today because I've been ill all week. I thought i would be able to get this memo done last night but when i was trying to work on it i ended up feeling real ill (I'll spare you the details) and wasn't able to do it. I've been trying real hard all day to get somethign done for you but I've basically just resulted in a huge failure and feeling even worse from stressing myself about this all day. I was hoping i would be able to work on this over the weekend and bring it to class on monday so i can at least get some sort of grade out of this. sorry again, and i hope you understand that i just had no idea how i was going to feel today and it just happened to take a turn for the worse.

sorry,

Shawn

Translation:

Professor Howell,

I'm sending you this email so late because I didn't think about it until 5 minutes ago. I skipped class on Wednesday because I was too high to leave my house. I also skipped class today because I was at black river with some bauch cats. I knew I wasn't going to be able to get this memo done but I didn't really care. I thought about working on it last night but I realized how hard it would be to type with a 40 of malt liquor taped to each of my hands. I've been getting high all day and making plans to go to Bill's hockey game, so its been real hard for me to fit this assignment into my schedule. I was hoping I would be able to get an extension on this because I am a huge waste of space and oxygen. Sorry for this, but I had no idea how bad of a student I was until today.

Sorry again,

Shawn

PLEASE DO NOT BOUNCE HEAD!

THANK YOU

DON'T ASK DON'T KNOW MORE INFo. In HAT

INFO IN HAT
FOUND by Arnie Rutkis

DEATH
FOUND by Julie Gerstein

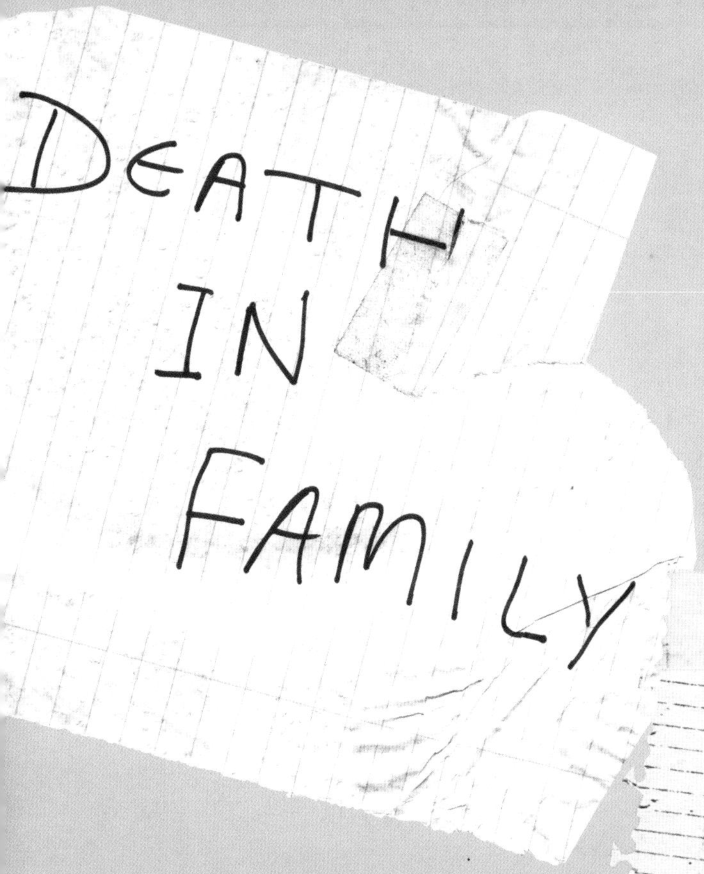

DEATH
IN
FAMILY

"A great way to avoid a parking ticket for a couple of hours..."
Davy

SCREENPLAY
FOUND by Cormac Symington

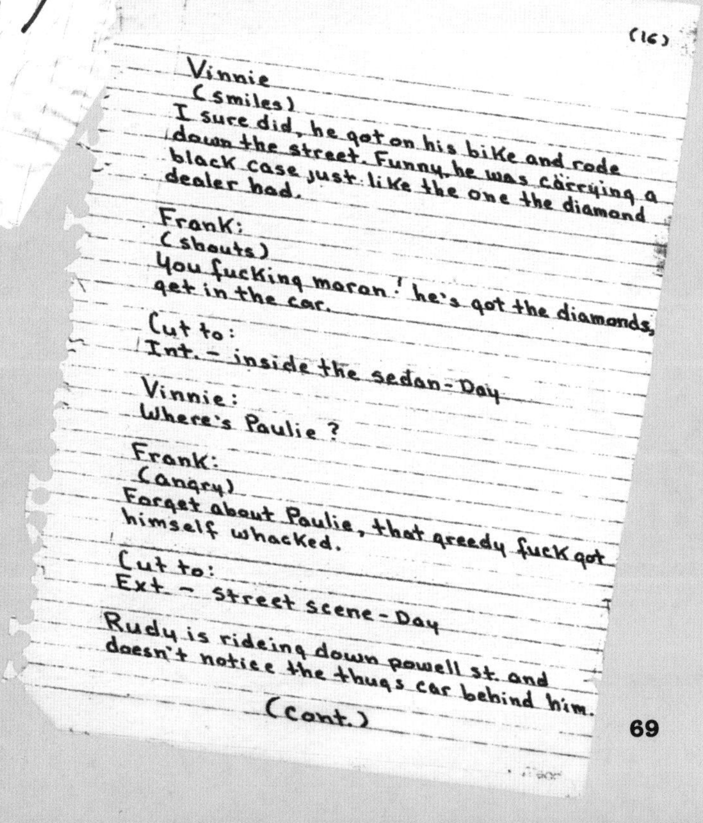

(16)

Vinnie
(smiles)
I sure did, he got on his bike and rode down the street. Funny, he was carrying a black case just like the one the diamond dealer had.

Frank:
(shouts)
You fucking moron! he's got the diamonds, get in the car.

Cut to:
Int. - inside the sedan - Day

Vinnie:
Where's Paulie?

Frank:
(angry)
Forget about Paulie, that greedy fuck got himself whacked.

Cut to:
Ext. - Street scene - Day

Rudy is rideing down powell st. and doesn't notice the thugs car behind him.

(Cont.)

Kayla,

Hey wuz up? OMG, yesterday I went to the ranch with Ashley and I have second thoughts about going to highschool in like 9 months. im not ready. Im so scared. Are you ready? Are you scared? yea I wanna get out of MSMS but wutz gonna happen when we get there? we might not all be together! Are we all still gonna be friends? Are we gonna have classes together? who are we gonna be friends with? what gonna happen? Is it the same as MSMS? We've never thought about this! Just promise me we'll always be friends!~ Well im hella tired so w/b/ASAP!

Valwayz,

Donna

AKA: Devil-
Child or
Bad Girl

SCARY
FOUND by Kim Finale

Erika Rioja

Erika we the boys want to know why are you going out with Nathan and you like all of us in a way. Tell us why and list how much you like the person with there name for example, Fred /not at all I think. Sorry for asking you all of these questions but we the boys want to know and get to the bottom of this. I'm always having to write the letters because they are some punks. You don't have to tell us right away but do tell us. Me, Fred, and Ricky thought of it, well it was really just Fred. All of the boys in the 6th grade likes you expect for some. That means that you are the finest girl in the whole 6th grade. A few them like you because of you know what but I don't. I like you because you have a pretty face/smile and your the only girl that has a little piece of hair going down your face. I think that makes you even prettier. You said that was your own style and I think that it's cool or whatever. That's all for now so I'll see you on the flip side, peace out.

P.S. Call me if you want to tell me about myself or just to talk about something. You know my number and if you don't then I'll tell you in your ear or something because I don't want any other girl but you to know my number. Not even Aisha

FOUND by Dave Hewitt

Mr. President,
I feel it is my obligation to express my views concerning your recent request to reinstate the draft registration. Every registration and draft in the past has pre-ceded military intervention. Please don't try to unify the country against the Russians to advance your own campaign. We need to talk with the Russians, not alienate them. We need to change our habits. Who ever gave us the right to the Persian Gulf? Don't let the military leaders plan a war that doesn't exits our freedom is not necessarily based on oil. If you had a choice between a human life and a can of oil, which would you choose?   Peace, Chris

Dear 1st Lady Bush,
Thankee so much for the Dand-ee-lion blusher!!! It was oh-so-lovely of you to think of me during these busy, topsy-turvy times ☺! You are a grrreat friend!
Chelsea Clinton
DELTA GAMMA, UNIVERSITY OF MICHIGAN

DAND-EE-LION
FOUND by Peter Rothbart

Christmas Revolution

Dear Santa,

Or should I just cut the crap and refer to you as the erotic poster boy of countless corporations that pimp you out so that their sales figures can climax on Christmas Eve. How many of your followers intoxicated with the instant gratification of all their bargain purchases' in which they refer to as 'Holiday Cheer', realize that your suit is red from the blood of children slaving away the rest of the year, without the luxury of holidays, in sweatshops around the world producing devices of leisure that within days will be forgotten by the obese spawn of the wealthy?

At first I wanted for your fat ass to get shot down by friendly fire when you fly over Iraq for your obligatory visit the troops this year. Then I realized that not only would the innocent reindeer get slaughtered but the western propaganda machine would spin the story to cast blame on the non-christian insurgency.

Instead, I hope that on Christmas Eve when you are terrorizing the world with your contractually circumnavigation of the earth, the Elves you hold captive in the north pole rise up and use their little hammers to smash the machines that you keep them chined to with substantiate wages that can barely afford a livelihood in the barren company town known as the North Pole. I want to see the sky light

EROTIC POSTER BOY
FOUND by Kirsty

MEMBER RULES
FOUND by David Meiklejohn

Article II, clause 7 (appended) - Member's Meetings

"If any member addresses problems regarding their relationship with a female during the course of a membership meeting, the remaining membership may elect to feel bad for them, son, provided the remaing membership can identify 99 problems of which a bitch ain't one."

Article II, clause 8 - Mystical Beasts

"Any member who causes a Mystical Beast to be present at a member meeting shall be solely responsible for feeding and housing the beast, as well as solely responsible for any damage or impairment of LLC assets caused by the beast. A mystical beast must have sweet wings, long talons, an unnatural ability to fly and/or ability to breathe fire or be declared a Mystical Beast by a court of applicable jurisdiction."

Article III, clause 5 - Wolf Shirts

"Unless agreed to in advance by all members, the LLC shall take no tax or legal advice from any person wearing a wolf shirt. A wolf shirt shall be defined as both depicting a wolf and being wicked sweet under applicable United Nations conventions or be declared wicked sweet in a US court of law with appropriate jurisdiction."

"I found a rain-soaked folder in the street that contained a 78-page legal document regarding the purchase of a coffee shop. It all looked pretty boring and I was about to pitch it into the recycling bin when these special clauses caught my eye. Watch out for them whales!"
David

74

Article IV, clause 11 - Allocation and Distribution of Liquidation Proceeds in the Event of Consumption by Whale:

"In the event that any member is consumed in whole by an animal of the order Cetacea, that member's share shall be liquidated and allocated among the other members in accordance with each member's percentage interest in the LLC. In the event that a member is consumed in part by an animal of the order Cetacea, a proportion of the member's capital account equal to the proportion of body mass of the member consumed shall be liquidated and allocated among the other members in equal portions."

Article V, clause 3 - Metal Hands

"Any member that should cause his natural hands to be removed intentionally and fashioned with metal hands without sound medical rationale shall have his membership rights frozen until such time as the remaining members accept and certify any applicable explanation for such action. This section shall not apply to members who, at the time of their admission into the LLC, bear metal hands."

Article V, clause 5 - Maritime Gross Negligence

"If a national maritime authority recognized by the International Maritime Authority finds that a member acted with gross negligence in the course of maritime action, the member shall surrender any membership interest involved in the action of the LLC. This provision does not apply to acts taking place in inland waters."

DAD:
You're Really Lucky
THAT THE SHIT you've
Been Spreading About
Me, Doesn't Really
Bother Me, But
IF I Hear Anymore
OF your Fuck'N
Lies ABout Me, TRust
Me I WILL BE BACK
To Drop your ASS.
I'm Not KiDDing

Not

I WILL NO LONGER
Be THE ScapegoAT
For THis FAMILies
Fucked up Life. I
Do Not WANT TO
Be CONTACTED By
ANyONe EVER
AGAin.
P.S. you DiD THis
Not Me, I WAS
VERy GOOD TO you
FiND you SHiT on
Me AGAIN, But Never
AGAin

SCAPEGOAT
FOUND by Taylor Hunter

THANKS
FOUND by Colleen Kennedy

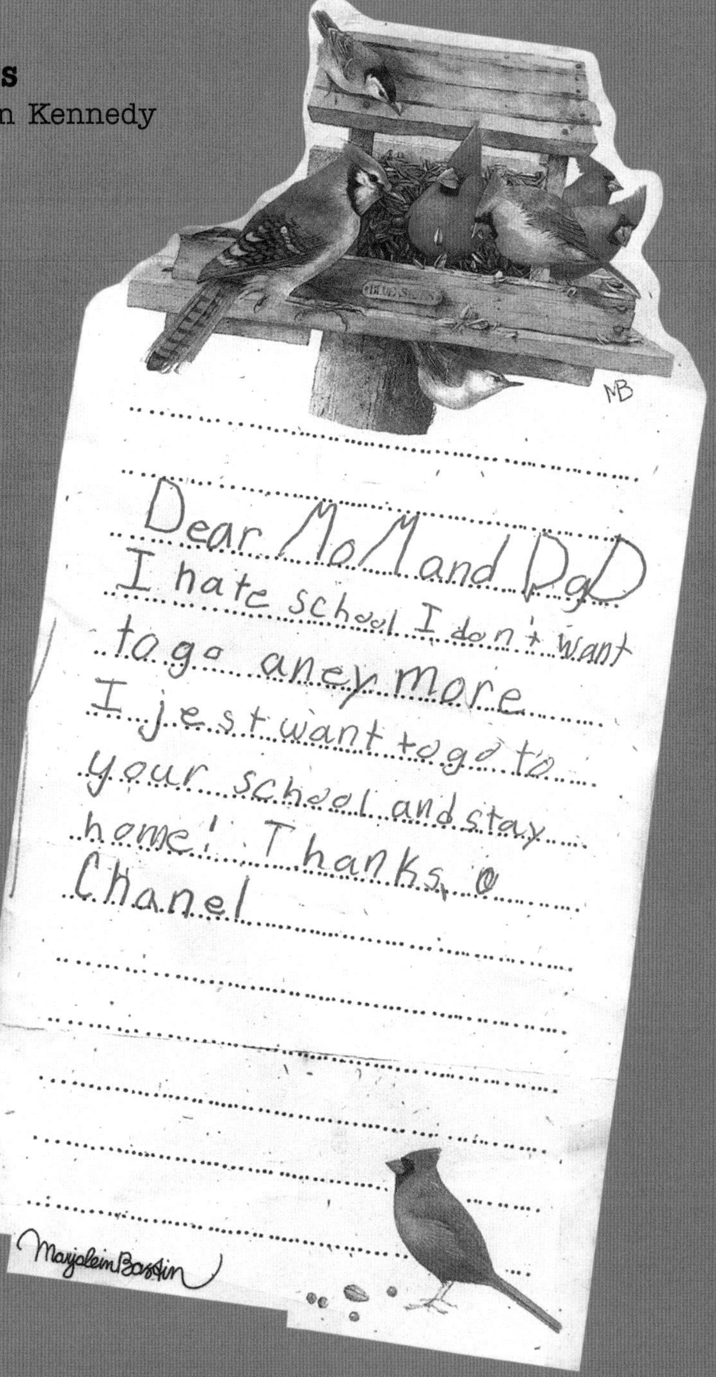

Dear MoM and DaD
I hate school I don't want
to go aney more
I jest want to go to
your school and stay
home! Thanks, o
Chanel

PASS
FOUND by David Kanthor

I'M going to 2nd grade. I hope I pass.

SCARCELY BE BOTH
FOUND by Claire Reichstein

You have to make up your mind
Mr. Dickens it was either the best
of time or the worst of time
it could scarcely be both, the
try was never ___ ___ and

HELP!

I urgently need to contact the young woman who looks similar to this drawing!

During the last week of June, she and her boyfriend, who I believe are students at U of T and Ryerson, applied to rent a one-bedroom apartment in my home. She told me they had to move because her mother, who was a superintendent of an apartment building, had to move to another location.

My house is located close to Queen St.W. & Elizabeth St.

(The apartment is the 2nd floor of my home, with a balcony off the kitchen, and a large backyard, and the apartment was advertised on www.Viewit.ca)

If they're still interested in the apartment, they don't have to pay first and last month's rent & NO RENT for the FIRST 5 MONTHS, then after that, I'd only ask them for $500 a month rent.

My phone number is:
(416) 385-48

I won't rent to anyone else but them, so, the apartment will remain unrented until I can contact this young woman and her boyfriend.

FRANTIC LANDLORD
FOUND by John Weidz

"My girlfriend and I found these plastered up all over the place on our evening walk. What the hell is the story here?" **John**

TAKE BETTER NOTES DAMMIT!

DAMMIT!
FOUND by Prentiss Riddle

Happy 30th kiddo. It gets better and better! Then it gets worse.

Love,

DE

WORSE!
FOUND by Sarah Heinemann

"Inside a copy of The DaVinci Code at a used bookstore." **Sarah**

WHATEVER
FOUND by Jenna and Mark

ESTᴰ 1880

THE LOS ANGELES
ATHLETIC CLUB

I'M OFFENDED THAT I'M REQUIRED to PEN SOME SORT OF "PROPPED UP" SENTIMENT. NONE THE LESS, YOU HAVE BEEN A GOOD FRIEND, SO HAPPY BIRTHDAY. WHATEVER, R.

STAN (opposite)
FOUND by Miriam

"I found this next to a dumpster." **Miriam**

do I still love him? I honestly don't know anymore. if you question love, doesn't that mean it's gone? I never question my love for my brother, even though he can be a huge pain, but maybe that's because he's been in my life forever...or maybe it's because I truly and deeply love him. I know I care immensely for **stan**; I'm anxious to talk to him after a hard day of work, and I like it when he comes over...at first. he gets here and suddenly I'm very tired or angry or other emotions that I haven't felt all day. I go about my day thinking of him often, but sometimes those thoughts turn to frustration or disgust if I think about him with **Dave**. I really don't have anything against **Dave**, except that I think that he's attractive to my boyfriend. it would be different if I were ignorant to their past together; knowing they are together all the time and touching and flirting just makes it hurt more. what if **stan** is subconsciously trying to replace me because I've grown tiresome and uninteresting? if he's is getting sick of me, that could almost be a relief because it would mean less heartbreak for both of us. listen to me, talking as if this is the end! I just don't want to give up, because it was so recently that I felt that this was IT, the real thing; it was only weeks ago, and that feeling urges me to keep trying to make it work..

he doesn't fit into my family; my relatives disgust him. knowing this changes what I say and how I behave because all I want is for him to be pleased with me.

I resent that he doesn't have a job, that a huge majority of his time is free time, that his life is largely problem free. I hate myself for even considering this, but sometimes I wonder if **stan** will end up getting what he wants in life largely because of who his father is.

my mom doubts he's "the one," and my dad seems to tolerate him, no more, because they don't have enough in common to become close. **stan** despises my mother, I think, though he'd never admit that to me. I think he finds my family's lifestyle somewhat "lower" than that of his family, and I know he doesn't mean to, but I feel he'll always be a rung higher on the sophistication ladder than me. which I shouldn't care about, I know, but **stan** makes dressing well and manners and politeness such a priority that somehow I get the feeling that I was brought up poorly or raised with no social graces. I know my parents did a great job with us. they love us to no end, have given us what we need, and have supported us in helping ourselves attain and achieve the rest. I should not be ashamed of the way I am, but, I can't help it—sometimes I am.

the lip piercing is another story, but I'm over it. some situations just require compromise. I'm willing to give in on some things. other things I am not.

case in point: I will not stay with a person who shows and vocalizes affection infrequently. I will not be in a relationship where sex is not often and pleasurable. physical affection is as important to me as personality compatibility. I need touches, kisses, smiles, caresses and "I love you"s, and, most of all, I need to be able to reciprocate all those and feel loved as well.

stan must know he's mostly my everything, and that sometimes his selflessness and generosity astonish me. he's very likely the smartest, most curious person I've ever been close to, and I've gained a lifetime's worth of knowledge in the nine months we've spent as a couple. he's integral in my life, and as much as I want to think I don't, I'm certain I need him, for better or worse. rage and frustration such as this rambling memo need an outlet, and perhaps when I find it, the boiling waters will calm and I'll be left with only a quiet, soothing warmth, enveloped in the arms of a man I'll never be able to forget.

HOLLYWOOD DREAM
FOUND by Chris Sullivan

"I work at a large record store in Toronto. We regularly find strange notes and lists that have been left behind; this one appeared today." **Chris**

I am not myself. I have become Vincent, an old classmate of mine from highschool and am appearing on television as part of a preview for an upcoming blockbuster film. On the screen, I am wearing a white suit there is grease in my hair and I am surrounded by a circular pattern of computer animated stars.

Watching the television is a six-foot tall banana with arms and legs sitting in a straight-backed timber chair. The banana stares on in silence, gets up stiffly and walks out the door.

BOY NAMED CHRIS
FOUND by Lori Sartin

"I found this deep in a couch at the community college where I take night classes." **Lori**

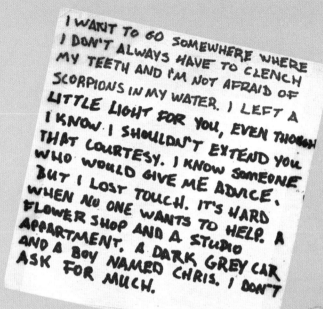

I WANT TO GO SOMEWHERE WHERE I DON'T ALWAYS HAVE TO CLENCH MY TEETH AND I'M NOT AFRAID OF SCORPIONS IN MY WATER. I LEFT A LITTLE LIGHT FOR YOU, EVEN THOUGH I KNOW I SHOULDN'T EXTEND YOU THAT COURTESY. I KNOW SOMEONE WHO WOULD GIVE ME ADVICE, BUT I LOST TOUCH. IT'S HARD WHEN NO ONE WANTS TO HELP. A FLOWER SHOP AND A STUDIO APPARTMENT. A DARK GREY CAR AND A BOY NAMED CHRIS. I DON'T ASK FOR MUCH.

mett me doaw by the big bush. from the kid whith the green Backpack

RENDEZVOUS
FOUND by Trevor Harris

Sue,

Hey hun,

Do you know this is exactly a year from the day Ash and I broke up. She walked out of my life, didn't look back, took the engagement ring didn't want anything to do with me any more, a year went bye not even a call, left her a message when grandma died nothing. I let it eat away at me for a year now, along with everything else I couldn't handle it any more. I loved her more then I loved life its self. She was the one for me the only one, but she got scared and let being scared win over how she really felt. Life isn't fair. I learned that the hard way to many time to hold on to any hope. I hope you don't hate me right now. I know you have all the reason in the world I promised I would call I promised I wouldn't try or succeed but I lied I just couldn't out of anyone I would hope you could understand that. If you can't I am sorry. I really don't know how to say this. You and I have bean friends since we were young, 3rd grade when you beat me in the 50 yard dash for gym. I was amazed that a girl could run as fast as us even faster. Do you remember the look on Dukes face not to mention Howie! thought he was going to drop dead right there. You have always bean one of a kind Sue. Ever since we met I new you were different I new you were going to be someone special in my life. Yes I new that at the age of 9. Hun, I have always loved you, for you the good the bad, the person you were and most important the great person you have become. I know when you get this I will be gone, that my plan to kill my self would have worked. I left this for Joel to give you once I was gone. I am sorry. I hope you can understand that I needed to go on to a better place now. My parents and I haven't bean getting a long, I still had a year of school no money to move out work sucked, after grandma Sadie died I felt like I lost my best friend, she was there no matter what thick or thin, I couldn't deal with it all any more. When I was in the hospital I tried that once to kill my self, I told them the day before they let me out I still wanted to die, but they thought I just wanted to stay in the hospital not go out and deal with the world. I know I am only 22 and I would have my life a head of me, I also know that if I would of called you I would still be a live right now, but please don't blame your self for this Sue, this is what I wanted this is how I wanted my life to end. I didn't want a be talked out of it, I know that you are hurting a lot right now, and I am sorry that I did this to you, but please no matter what your feeling right now don't follow in my foot steps. My family has lost grandma Sadie and now me, I know they would be devastated to hear they lost you to, as would your family, if things get hard think of you beautiful nieces and how you need to be there for Betty's surgery. Look at all the good your meant to do in the world. You are meant for greater things that's why God wouldn't let you die when you wanted to the times you tried almost succeeded her pulled you back, this was my time to go, I don't want a see you in hell. Live life be happy and live each day to the fullest. Know I always loved you and always will.

Love
Eric

Phil,

I found this charm in the candle your mom gave me - after our conversation today - tonight I feel like its some sort of sign - and I feel better about things - so I'm hoping it will do the same for you. (I know, I'm silly)

I'm thinking about you, wondering what your doing right now, whatever it is - I want to be doing it with you, almost anything anyway. Its late, so I'm thinking your probably sleeping. I miss sleeping with you, although my bed smells much better and I get some covers, and theres never smelly socks under my pillow. Oddly enough, I even miss those things. Well, I'm going to bed soon - I miss you always - and love you with all my heart!

Kristy

THINKING ABOUT YOU
FOUND by Elizabeth Crane

Dear FOUND magazine,

I'm not sure this qualifies as a FOUND item since the actual things I found were returned to their rightful owner. However, I've enclosed the thank you letter I received, which turned out to be almost as good as the goods themselves. Here's the story.

Upon looking for a map to the LA airport as we drove out of Joshua Tree National Park, my friend Eric and I happened upon a stash of someone's personal belongings in the glove compartment or our rental car. At first, I noticed a pair of tan leather gloves sticking out from a small stack of papers. (Wow. Who actually keeps gloves in a glove compartment!?) How sad, I thought, the last renter had left her church gloves behind, never to be worn again. But as I rifled through the Budget-rent-a-car documents, I began to uncover a handful of other personal things. I put them all in my lap and sorted through them delicately, fascinated by this odd collection of items which included the following:

- A wad of coupons collected from all sorts of places, paper-clipped together
- A tiny cloth change purse, which held a tube of used-up lipstick, some mismatched buttons, a foreign coin, and a few small seashells
- A stack of mail, all addressed to Kay "Jones" (not actual name), Joshua Tree, CA. Some of it was junk mail, but there were also some unpaid utility bills.

Then I struck gold. There was a handwritten letter in an envelope. I felt guilty opening it — this was someone's private letter after all — but my curiosity got the better of me. The words, written in a swoopy (yet sloppy) cursive, just about broke my heart.

"Dearest Brother,
I heard you was having a hard time with money and I know I don't have much, but maybe this twenty dollars will help out.
Your Loving Sister, Kay."

This woman - who saved coupons for laundry detergent and had a pile of overdue bills - was sending her brother twenty dollars. The letter was complete and the envelope had been addressed, but there was no money in it.

Well, it was a done deal. We decided to send this woman her belongings (so she could use her coupons, pay her bills, hold onto her seashells, and send that letter) — after all, we had her full name and address. And we'd been so touched by that letter she'd written, we decided to include some money for her brother. Once I returned to Chicago, I put everything in a padded envelope - along with a humble little note of explanation and a twenty-dollar bill - and took it to the post office.

A month later, this letter arrived in the mail. I treasure it - every word (especially the "wept for about 3 to 5 minutes" part). Kay and I now write each other on occasion - she even sent me some photographs of her dogs (enclosed).

RETURNED THINGS
FOUND by Meredith Siemsen and Eric Roberts

"Do we ever return FOUND stuff that's sent in to us to its original owners? Occasionally if the items seem especially important and the owners are easily identifiable. Here's a story I really love of a find being returned."

Davy

3/12/02

Hi you two receive the return of my things on 3-9-02 I set in my bed at about 8:00 PM reading my mail then I looked at the big envelope and said who do, I knew in Chicago then I said no one opening the package and Pulling out the zip lock bag and seeing my things and your letter and the twenty dollar bill I set in my bed and Wept for about 3 to 5 minutes Praise God on high. how He had use you honest and godly people to return my things which was not anygood to anyone but me and then you the two of you to donated the money to someone you had never seen nat told to. I knew God hands was all in this no one but children of God would have done what you two did, I love you two, Please keep me and my family in your Prays who knows maybe God will make it so that one day We might meet that would be a blessing Please Keep in Touch if You Will my Phone number is 760-___ address 87.___ Joshua Tree Ca 92252 would love to become Pen Pal (over)

P.S. I Pray God Will multiply back 100 foes in return to the Two of you. gave this testament in Church on Sunday 3/10/02 Thanks Kay

GETTING TO KNOW YOU BEFORE I FUCK YOU
APPLICATION

Personal
Name_____ AGE__ D.O.B_____

_____ Phone_____

Address_____

Do you have boyfriend/girlfriend yes or no_____)
(If yes is it the person you having sex with now_____)

How do you like it fast, medium, or slow? _____

*Fast is it rough and hard.
*Medium is you like to take your time but still like it rough.
*Slow is when you wont to take your time and make sure you are
doing it right.

How low can you go? _____

Do you like to have four play before you have sex? _____

Do you know where there spot is? _____

How long will you last? _____

WHEN YOUR FINISH RETRUN TO THE PERSON THAT GAVE IT
TO YOU.

I _____ list all the following information above is
the truth the whole truth and nothing but the truth.

NOTE Any information you gave above in not true you
will be severely punish. You will be fine and sent to jail

HOW DO YOU LIKE IT?
FOUND by Pat Kambitsch

"I found this in a high school." **Pat**

PIRATE
FOUND by Mike DiBella

Are you a pirate?

Do you enjoy swashbuckling, plundering, and generally being a scourge of the seven seas? Then you're probably not interested in renting a room in a two bedroom apartment for only 400 bucks a month, deposit is just two hundred and fifty, all the utilities are paid for, its within walking distance of a grocery store, next to seven buslines, and there four different ethnic restaraunts in the area! That and the guy looking for the roommate isn't a jerk. Seriously, I've ran polls on this and people have confirmed I'm not a jerk. If your interested call 742-71 ̄ ̄, if you just want to give me money for some reason, call 742-71 ̄ ̄. If you just want to cuddle, call someone else.

If you decide that you love me anytime today Please call me

ANYTIME
FOUND by Anna Caramanna

91

EVER CUT YOUR SKIN FOR FUN?
SELL YOUR ASS?!
SLEEP ON THE STREET?
DO YOU LIKE PAIN? TAKE HEROIN?
IF SO LETS START A BAND
CALL 246-0882 AND
LEAVE A MESSAGE WITH
INNOCENT BYSTANDER JESSE

BAND NEEDED
FOUND by Katherine Raz

Happy Fathers day to you, even though you told me I can't cook and the pie I made sucked.

Happy fuckin valintimes day you fat ass bitch.

P.S. I didn't think you needed any more candy

ANY MORE CANDY
FOUND by Sara Nowak

WHEN YOUR DONE
FOUND by Dylan Strzynski

Goals

1. Go to church. Find God, than find myself through him. Get Baptised.

2. Party a lot. Meet new people. Start drinking once a week. Be Social. My Mom met my Dad at a party... Don't forget that.

3. Start exercising with my Mom this week (March 10th - March 14th)

4. Spend a lot of time alone. Find myself. Figure out a way to be happy alone. I need to know that I can be content by myself. I know that I am beautiful. I know that I have a wonderful personality. I know that I'm smart. I know that I'm worthy of being loved.

5. Find a new Job. Tomorrow, I will call back all places that I applied to. I will turn all my applications into new places.

6. Go to the 200 Bar alone; get soaked into the music. Go to a lot of small concerts alone.

7. Take one class at SCC on March 31st. Debt Free Living. $45 Sec:SA. Monday, March 31, 2003. 7-10 pm Rm A-1. Inst: Meyer.

8. Go home and visit w/ family more often At least 3x/week.

DON'T FORGET THAT
FOUND by Fil Lincoln

"I went to take out the trash and found this in the bushes." **Fil**

KARATE KID

FOUND by Karin Rabe and Matt Gaffron

"This sign was hanging on all the mailboxes at our apartment complex. It was obvious to us that this poor kid was just writing down exactly what his parents had said to him. I think I actually know which kid this is — he's about 10 or 11 years old. I'm happy to say I've seen him playing outside since he had to post this sign so I figure either his karate staff was returned or his parents relented and he's no longer grounded." **Karin and Matt**

Lost...

This is a karate staff. It is a piece of equipment meant for training . I was not suppose to play with it outside but disobeyed my parents. Now I have lost it and am grounded until it is re-turned. Please help.

Benjamin

Lost the 2nd week in January. If found please return to #3455 or call 713-393-63

PEN CAP
FOUND by Mike Rosenthal

SHAME ON YOU
FOUND by Lev

I NEED A MIRACLE!

≡ HUGE REWARD ≡

On July 4th, AT 7:30 P.M. I accidentally left a shopping bag filled with my babies (my favorite dolls) on christopher + Bleecker st.

I really miss them, they are like children to me.

Please call (212) ____
OR (201) ____

CONTACT

____ christopher st. N.Y.

I am desperate to see them again please help!

REWARD: $150.00

On Friday July, 4th, I lost a bag of dolls. Someone found them and returned all the dolls to me except for 1 doll that he gave to someone at the STONEWALL BAR. The doll was a chucky doll.

If anyone has this doll I will pay $150.00 for his return.

Please call (212) ____

Thank you so much!

I miss the little guy.

Helen loves me more than I love her. ♡

Bobby's love a comparent Helen's love

100

FOREBODING
FOUND by Dave L

"This living will was nestled in the pages of an Adolf Hitler biography." **Dave**

7-18-99

I have had a sense of foreboding regarding this trip for some time. I have been left with the impression that I shall not return from it... in this lifetime. Understand that if I am taken it is somehow necessary and should be viewed as merely a delay. I have prepared myself for the journey, do not fear because I am indestructible.

My possessions do not mean a great deal to me only my work. However, I would like 2,000 dollars from my savings given to Rita Brau with the hope that someone will also explain my feelings to her. The balance of my money should be given to Brian Keith Lennigan for the purpose of completing the mission.

All of my rifles and ammunition should also be transferred to Brian Lennigan as well as my writings. All handwritten manuscripts, computer disks, printed copies and electronic copies of both *The Immortal Remains* and *Vae Victis* should be transferred to him on the condition that he finishes the manuscript to the best of his ability. Save for spelling and grammatical corrections the text should be left unaltered. I regret more than anything not finishing this text. One half of all proceeds from their publication should go to help poor and hungry people throughout the world and the other half should be split between Tess Emczek and Brian Lennigan with the hope that he receives a formal education.

The rest of my possessions can be split up in any way seen fit under the provision that Evelyn Santelli and her family in no way receive anything and do not profit by my passing. For legal reasons I have explicitly stated this.

I retract and ask apology for any bad remarks made about any people or groups except for Barbara Allison Jo Devereaux and her family who have forever earned my enmity and for whom I may return.

I make these statements in full control of my rational faculties and in complete mental and physical health.

Jon Leo Trespian

101

GREETINGS!
FOUND by Matt Stilt

Hello Bonehead –

Now that you have completely fucked up the program and alienated everyone since firing me, you should know what the hell is going on.

Your idiotic decisions have lead to the demise of a great team. You have not got the slightest idea how to manage a team and never will you stupid fuckweasel.

To give you an idea of how little you know about what the fuck is going on – try dialing up your own office phone and when your shitbum voice comes on the answering device, punch in '0505' and then punch in '1' followed by '1' and then when some important message comes on, (like someone who wants to join you worthless program) punch in the number '0' and it will be erased!. I'll bet you didn't know that you fucking moron! I have been doing that for the past six months!

I went to see a voodoo lady recently and paid with $$ from your team to have her put a hex on your pitiful life. Be prepared for a scrotum infection that slowly, painfully and irreversibly creeps up your ass to the point where you shit fire continuously until your balls disintegrate culminating in your dick shriveling up and falling off!!

So while you still have a dick, go take a flying fuck at a rolling donut you shitpig cop!

Have a nice day, fuckwit!

From you know who.

P.S. Why don't you take a flying fuck at the moon too!!

40

SLEEP ON THE COUCH
FOUND by Richard Wilson

Gary —

Please sleep on the couch. We'll talk in the morning. Coleen

J + Steven = L-O-V-E

LOVE P.S. He comes over every Wed. Night →

AND WE Really do have it, that's why I'm 15 + pregnant

WE REALLY DO HAVE IT
FOUND in a church hallway by Candice Morey

Art and Architecture

The setting is a dance. The characters are in their late teens. The dance could be in at a frat party, high school dance, or college formal. The three characters are seated on a couch. An attractive girl in a prom dress sits between two guys may be in either are all in semi-formal attire, the girl is in a prom dress and the two guys sits down to talk with each other. One of the guys is dating the girl and the other guy is a good friend of the girl, although the two guys have only briefly met on prior occasions.

Erica- Sweet and worldly girl, very intelligent

Kevin – Erica's boyfriend, gregarious

Jared – Erica's friend, comic but intelligent

Erica: I am so glad you could ~~make it~~ Come to the dance today Kevin.

Kevin: You had doubts that I ~~wouldn't make it?~~ Couldn't come?

Jared: She has been talking about you all week!

Jared: ~~She has been talking about you all week!~~ much ~~like me~~ you would be

Erica: Well,if you didn't see the person you loved that much like me you would be excited to.

Kevin: I don't think he has that problem.

Jared: Yes I am not jumping to bang the pots and pans like some people.

Kevin: What?

Jared: Well, Erica and I have been having some interesting conversations about ... extra curricular activities.

Kevin: Oh has she?

Erica: Well there is not much to tell.

Kevin and Jared: Not much to tell?!?

All: *Laugh*

Erica: Well actually we were talking about other related topics not focusing on us.

Kevin: Like what?

Jared: Poly-amorous relationships, menage trois, threesomes.

Kevin: Is this a statement or a request.?

Erica: Neither!

Jared: I was just saying that they didn't happen that much I didn't think. I mean it never really came to my mind before. Just not something I have spent much thought on. Your girlfriend has quite an active imagination.

Kevin: That's for sure.

Erica: Well it happens more than you think.

Jared: No…

Kevin: Actually it does.

Pause

All: *Laugh uneasily.*

Jared: Well I don't know what to say.

Kevin: Well you have already said a lot for someone who has not put much thought into this.

Jared: Is that a statement or a request?

Pause

All: *Laugh uneasily*

Erica: Well before you two guys drop your pants I have tell you it would be a bit of crime to do this…in fact a felony. *Laughs* And besides I am tired. Can we go now Kevin? This has been such a funny conversation I hate to leave you Jared. It is always great to talk to you…never a dull moment.

Jared: Yes it has been quite stimulating. I hope you two have fun without me.

All: *Laugh*

105

All rise. Jared hugs Erica. Jared and Kevin exchange a hardy handshake. They all part ways.

DESCRIPTION
Found by Popcorn Pete

"Perform this play with friends. And if anyone finds page 3, please send it in." **Pete**

"This is one of my favourite finds of all time." **Davy**

TEACHER-COURSE EVALUATION

Also, write comments for items on both the front and back side of the sheet. Examples of possible topics are given for each item; use them or <u>any</u> others that are relevant. Include strengths and weaknesses, as appropriate.

1) COURSE *Comments* (e.g., content, structure, approach, educational value) OF A SPECIFIC CLASS

I CAN NOT REMEMBER ANYTHING ABOUT THE CONTENT ~~OF THE~~ RECALL THE MOST BORING MOMENTS ANY MORE THAN I COULD ~~FORGET~~ THE MOST BORING MOMENTS OF MY LIFE. THE EDUCATIONAL VALUE WAS SO PHENOMENALLY LOW THAT MY FRUSTRATION GREW INTO HATRED FOR HER, AND THEN IT BECAME MORE WIDESPREAD, AFFECTING MY FAMILY AND FRIENDS AND POSSIBLY PEOPLE I HAVE NEVER MET BEFORE UNTIL I FINALLY REACHED THE POINT WHERE ~~I HATED MYSELF FOR~~ ~~EVEN EVER~~ BEING THERE.

(e.g., content, structure, approach, educational value)

structure ?? which one?
no educational value
He learned nothing
One-sided introduction to NYC. – Only Beth's view
the quest lectures were sometimes interesting – only interesting thing

8) ADJECTIVE What adjective best describes this course? ___HORRIFYING___

6) EVALUATION METHODS (e.g., the educational value of tests, papers, homework)
The papers were obviously intended as thought exercises, and they succeeded passing well as such, but what they had to do with any of the other papers, readings, presentations, or discussions is quite beyond me. In fact, what <u>any</u> paper, reading, presentation, or discussion had to do with any other paper, reading, presentation or discussion, or the ostensible program topics, is an issue which has yet to be clarified.

___N METHODS (e.g., the educational value of tests, papers, homework)
HER RATHER NON-INSPIRED EVALUATION OF OUR PAPERS; BUT I CAN'T BLAME HER FOR ANYTHING EXCEPT FOR THE IDIOTIC TOPICS SHE REQUIRED US TO WRITE ABOUT.

3) INTELLECTUAL STIMULATION *Comments* (e.g., amount and type of thinking you did)
~~Bullshit~~ "Bullshit" is the only word I can think of, excuse my French. She didn't try to stimulate, and the material didn't stimulate me. When it came time to write papers, I made bullshit up because I didn't care one way or the other.

5 = excellent

6) EVALUATION METHODS (e.g., the educational value of tests, papers, homework)
I have no idea how I'm being evaluated.

HORRIFYING
FOUND by Jesse B

106

5 3) **INTELLECTUAL STIMULATION**
Comments (e.g., amount and type of thinking you did) WHEN HER TWENTY-FIVE POUND CAT CLAWED ME IN THE GENITALS.

CLASSROOM DYNAMICS Circle term for type of course: **lecture / seminar / lab / other =** _____
(e.g., given this type of course, assess student participation, interest level, discussions, peer review)

There basically was no dynamic. Students not showing up, coming excessively late, and sleeping, that was the dynamic.

9) **ADDITIONAL COMMENTS**

a note about the cats: the litterbox was in the bathroom. It contained, well, cat shit. one of the less repulsive substances known to the human race. If the instructor hadn't wanted us in the bathroom, she could have selected a less unpleasant method of signalling it.

4 = good

7) **CLASSROOM DYNAMICS** Circle term for type of course: **lecture /** (**seminar**) **/ lab / other =** _____
(e.g., given this type of course, assess student participation, interest level, discussions, peer review)

At times, it seemed that if someone were to begin speaking in tongues, we all would have nodded and pretended that it was an insightful comment, just because someone had actually SAID something

7) **CLASSROOM DYNAMICS** Circle term for type of course: **lecture / seminar / lab / other =** _____
(e.g., given this type of course, assess student participation, interest level, discussions, peer review)

TWO DAYS A WEEK I POUCHED OFF CATHAIR" TO HER UNINSPIRED, ANTIQUATED BABBLE ABOUT ART THEORY, AND IF I was LUCKY—I COULD CHEW ON A STALE BAGEL THAT I PAID OVER TWENTY THOUSAND DOLLARS FOR.

L 3) **INTELLECTUAL STIMULATION**
Comments (e.g., amount and type of thinking you did)

Some, came out of irritation forceful confrontation with the subject.

1 = poor

2 3) **INTELLECTUAL STIMULATION**
Comments (e.g., amount and type of thinking you did)

Ummm... I frequently contemplated my watch during class. Sometimes I would speculate as to what Ben Daniels or Dave Kurtz looked like, since they never came to class.

BUNNY
FOUND by Peter Rothbart

WHOLE FOODS
Customer Communication

Please take a moment to give us your comments, suggestions or questions. If you need a personal or confidential reply please include your phone number.

Date:

The bunny or rabbit are ~~scribble~~ stupid get rid of them.

Response: I am not sure what bunny or rabbit you refer to here. Please be more specific. Thanks.

Team Member Name: David Lott
Store Team Leader
Date: 2/13/01

BELIEVER
FOUND by Jessie Henderson

I can't belive my step farther belive's in <u>Satian</u>

108
BEST FOR A WHILE...
FOUND by Elizabeth Berry

I unplugged the T.V.
I think it's best for a while...

NO MORE SLEEPOVERS
FOUND by David Allison

Dear claire
Happy birthday. I am
sorry that i frgot your
birthday. I would like to be
your frend agaien but we would
not have anny sleepovers. Here
is a present

MARRIAGE PPRS.

Divorce Papers

Use blanks below or
unprinted sides for
your own headings.

WASTE NOT
FOUND by Mike Smith

"Someone gave me an old filing cabinet. Many of the old files still
had tabs on them. When I pulled them out to replace them I
found that written on the back of the one labelled 'Divorce
Papers' were the words 'Marriage PPRS. Funny how easy things
can change. Funny... and horrible at the same time." **Mike**

SEAT 29E
FOUND by Alex Wagner

Dear _____ Airlines,

I am disgusted as I write this note to you about the miserable experience I am having sitting in seat 29E on one of your aircrafts. As you may know, this seat is situated directly across from the lavatory, so close that I can reach out my left arm and touch the door.

②
All my senses are being tortured simultaneously. Its difficult to say what the worst part about sitting in 29E really is? Is it the stench of the sanitation fluid that is blown all over my body every 60 seconds when the door opens? Is it the wooosh of the constant flushing? OR is it the passengers asses that seem to fit into my personal space like a pornographic jig-saw puzzel?

③
I constucted a stink-shield by shoving one end of a blanket into the overhead compartment - while effective in blocking at least some of the smell, and offering a small bit of privacy, the ass-on-my-body factor has increased, as without my evil glare, passengers feel free to lean up against what they think is some kind of blanketed wall. The next ass that touches my shoulder will be the last!

④ I am picturing a board room full of executives giving props to the young promising engineer that figured out how to squeeze an additional row of seats onto this plane by putting them next to the LAV.

29E

I would like to flush his head in the toilet that I am close enough to touch from my seat. , and taste,

⑤ Putting a seat here was a very bad idea. I just heard a MAN GROAN in there! THIS SUCKS!

29E

DEPICTION OF MANS BUTT IN MY FACE.

Worse yet, I've paid over $400.00 for the honor of sitting in this seat!

⑥ Does your company give refunds? I'd like to go back where I came from and start over. Seat 29E could only be worse if it were inside the bathroom. was located

I wonder if my clothing will retain the sanitizing odor.... what about my hair! I feel like I'm bathing in a toilet bowl of blue liquid, and there is no man in a little boat to save me.

I am filled with a deep hatred for your plane designer and a general dis-ease that

⑦ May last for hours.

We are finally decending, and soon I will be able to tear down the stink-shield, but the scars will remain.

I suggest that you initiate immediate removal of this seat from all of your crafts. Just remove it, and leave the smouldering brown hole empty, for a good place for sturdy/non-absorbing luggage maybe, but not human cargo.

Signed, Passenger #29E

111

DRAW HIS PICTURE HERE
FOUND by Davy Rothbart

NOT TO BE WORSHIPPED
FOUND by Kirsten G

SOBER
FOUND by Rachel Jacobs

Dear Jesus,

Thank you for not making me cut my dick off
and suck yours. Today I am one cool sober
mother fucker.

Amen

SANTA'S
NAME IS NOT WRITTEN
IN THE BIBLE BUT
SATAN IS.
NOW MOVE THE LETTER
N IN SANTA AND PLACE
IT ON THE END OF HIS
NAME AND NOW YOU
HAVE SATAN.
AN IDOL NOT TO BE
WORSHIPPED.

"I found this slip of paper in a copy of What to
Expect when you're Expecting that I borrowed
from Bernal Heights Library in San Francisco."
Rachel

A MYSTERY AT A TIME
FOUND by Marit Nelson

"I found this handmade sign
taped to a locked door in a
deserted alley." **Marit**

STDs

Solving One Mystery At A Time...

,11/15/00,

From: "
To: <_____@neu.com>
Subject:
Date: Wed, 15 Nov 2000 19:51:06 -0000
X-Priority: 3

<u>aram</u> ...if this is <u>aram</u>. e-mail me. in ireland. homeless.

A GOOD POSITION AND A
COMFORTABLE SALARY
WILL BE YOURS
NEVER !
02 13 17 25 28 51

Ms. Casale,

I feel very awkward,
but your underware is
showing greatly.

— Brittani

HEY GROUCHY!

DON'T call me til ~~xxxx~~
You have good news about my lines,
the Goonies, and Rhode Island, well —
any 2 of the 3.

Later Dude!

ANY 2 OF THE 3
FOUND by Tyrone White

I'M Sorry about last friday... I thaght It was you!! I Swear

I'm Really Sorry about Saturday.

Reasons **NOT** to love me:
I'm an ass hole ☑
I slept w/ your Best friend ☑
I never pay ☑
Opening doors is for wussies ☑
I'm clingy (really, you may <u>need</u> scotch guard!!!) ☑
I HATE CHILDREN ☑
P.S. I want to build a life together.

"I found these notes nailed to trees on the way from my house to the subway. The first tree explained Friday, the second Saturday, and the third had the handy checklist." **Sindhu**

THE RAILING

FOUND by William Seebring via email

On Mon, 5 May 2003 15:52:49 EDT ⸻ @aol.com writes:

Dear Peter:

I have the arrival for 10 days two very active!!!!! children. 4 years old and 6 years old on June 20.

As mentioned, I am very concerned about not having the stair railing up for the protection of any accidents happening --- one of them sleepwalks.

So, what is the status of the railing and will I be able to have it in by then.

Thea

On Mon, 5 May 2003 16:36:25 EDT ⸻@juno.com writes:

probably not. work load is just too tight. I suggest you rig in some straps for the kids at night - I have some old cat collars you could use - they'd work, on their ankles is what I mean. Secure the other end to the bedpost and the kids won't get far.

no house is accident free. Least you're not living in a houseboat. Know what I mean?

Peter

On Tue, 6 May 2003 12:32:05 EDT ⸻@aol.com
<mailto:⸻@aol.com> writes:

Peter:

What will I have by the end of June?

Thea

"William received an email from a woman named Thea that was clearly intended for someone else. William decided to write back as if he were the guy she was trying to write to! What followed was one of the more hilarious email exchanges I've ever seen — the ethics may be unsound, but the results are tremendous." **Davy**

On Tue, 6 May 2003 15:30:36 EDT ◌◌◌◌@juno.com writes:

I don't know. Maybe a greater appreciation for the uncertainty of
life. Life is a struggle. I can tell you that. We plow, we sow
but what do we reap? A few shiny trinkets to hang on our walls?
Debt out the wazoo. I tell you, Thea, I am tired. I just want to
sit down somewhere with a bag of peanuts. In their shells. No
salt. I can't handle the salt. But I would like that. I really
would. Maybe "I'll" have that by the end of June. Does that help?

Peter

On Wed, 7 May 2003 09:19:04 EDT ◌◌◌◌@aol.com
<mailto:◌◌◌◌@aol.com> writes:

No, Peter and I am not appreciating your non-professional-unbusiness-like
replies. I also lead a very tiring hectic life (as do many other people)---it is
todays world.

My point is that you have had the commission for over a year at this
time. If you have taken on too many projects, I don't feel I should have to
"suffer" for it. So, let's get serious about this thing and get on with it.

I have two small children and my mother (who is blind) coming within
the next three months and I would like to have some actual timing down on
this thing. Your solution with putting up "straps" of some sort would not
prevent anything and I don't think it is funny. I am especially concerned
about the safety of my mother who is just adjusting to no sight and relies
on physical guidance of walls and railings to get around in strange places.

Sorry, I don't relate to your cavalier answers. There is no humor at this
point.

Thea

On Wed, 7 May 2003 13:46:37 EDT ◌◌◌◌@juno.com writes,

Thea,

They say humor is a relative thing. Perhaps this time, "they" are right.

Peter

On Wed, 7 May 2003 14:32:57 EDT E_____@aol.com
 <mailto:E_____@aol.com> writes:

Dear Peter:

Stop all work on the project.

My attorney, Samuel Reuben will be contacting you regarding deposits.

I feel your irresponsible replies to my "serious" requests have made
working with you no longer feasible.

Thea

On Wed, 7 May 2003 17:54:47 EDT _____@juno.com writes:

Thea,

Not only has your attorney contacted me but, in fact, Sammy is here
with me now.

On my sofa.

Eating peanuts.

You see, Thea, Sammy and I have been "seeing" each other for some
time. Since last May. The eleventh, actually. It was a Saturday.
 In fact, you introduced us. Do you remember? It all seemed so
incidental then. Why wouldn't it? But now you know the truth. Not
many people do. Not even Sheila. Well, she may suspect it. Dottie
knows. I think. She said something the other day that made me think
she does. Anyway, suffice to say that I'm making some changes in my
life. I have thrown my tool belt and my plane and my Skil saw into the
culvert that runs along Delshire Boulevard. Don't bother retrieving
them. They are gone. I am going to cultivate cheeses. Sammy will help
me on the exporting end. Those are my plans. I'm sorry about the
railing. Please don't hate me.

Peter

NON-SMOKER
FOUND by Maggie G

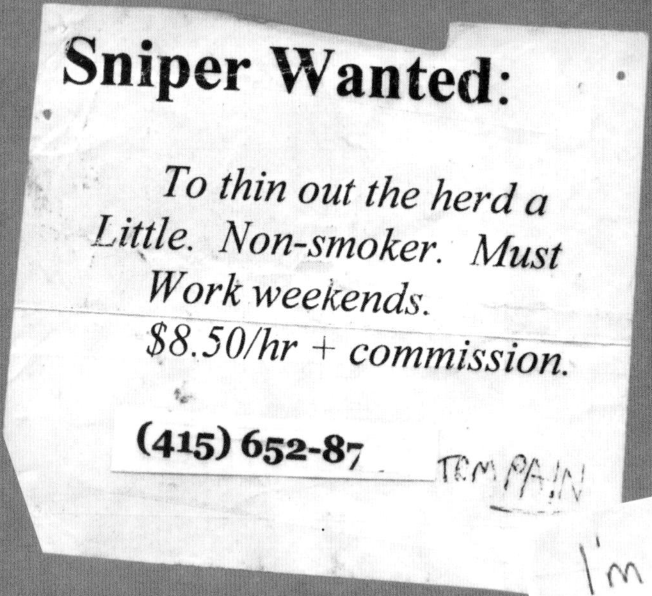

Sniper Wanted:

To thin out the herd a Little. Non-smoker. Must Work weekends. $8.50/hr + commission.

(415) 652-87

TEM PAIN

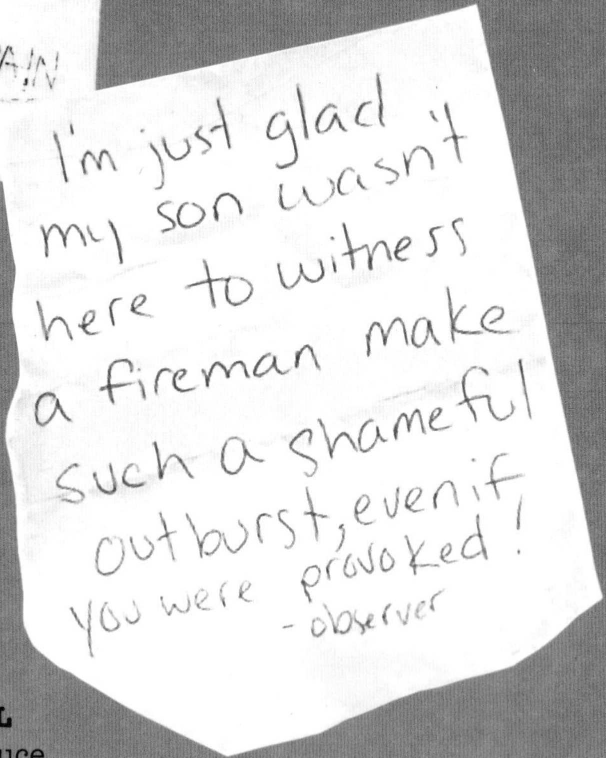

I'm just glad my son wasn't here to witness a fireman make such a shameful outburst, even if you were provoked!
- observer

SHAMEFUL
FOUND by Bruce

```
MONTHLY BUDGET

RENT          600.

CELL PHONE 50.
TELEPHOE    50

ELEC/Gas    45.

CABLE       60.

Bus/TAXI    60

FOOD        500.
LIQUOR      600 INCL BArs  ($20.00 per DAY)

LAUNDRY     30

CRACK       600

ATTORNEY 250

MISC        250.
ASVINGS   100

TOTAL INCOME NEEDED    $ 3195.00

         YEARLE INCOME NEEDED  $ 38,220.00
```

MONTHLY BUDGET
FOUND by Lea McKenny Willcox

SOCKS
FOUND by Gulliver Gold

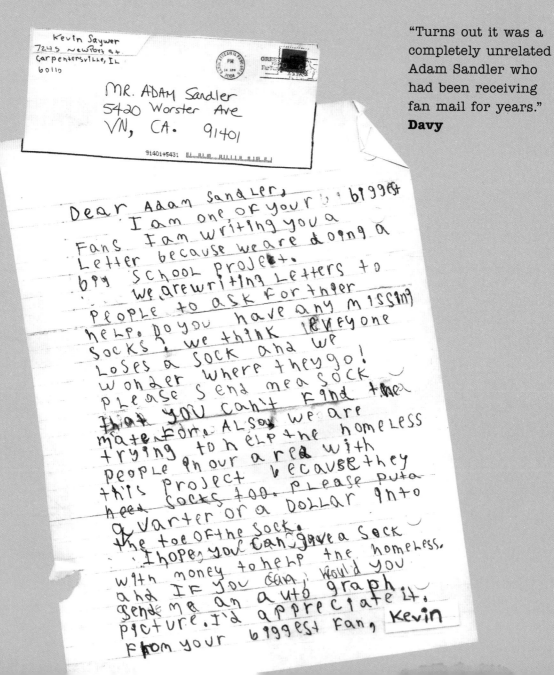

Kevin Saywer
7245 Newport St
Carpentersville, IL
60110

MR. ADAM Sandler
5420 Worster Ave
VN, CA. 91401

91401+5431

"Turns out it was a completely unrelated Adam Sandler who had been receiving fan mail for years."
Davy

Dear Adam Sandler,
  I am one of your biggest Fans. I am writing you a Letter because we are doing a big school project. we are writing letters to people to ask for their help. Do you have any missing socks? we think everyone loses a sock and we wonder where they go! Please send me a sock that you can't find the mate for. Also we are trying to help the homeless people in our area with this project because they need socks too. Please put a quarter or a dollar into the toe of the sock.
  I hope you can give a sock with money to help the homeless. and IF you can, would you send me an auto graph picture. I'd appreciate it.
From your biggest fan, Kevin

"I wish someone had clued me in to all of this when I was younger – it might have saved me a whole lotta turmoil!" **Davy**

Remember

To always listen to what ever the elder has to say, wether Its Dumb shit or If Ihris right. Because their always right at least thats how they feel and todds alot of the times they are right and alot of times their not, but the point is you cant ever change how they think, because your young and Ignorants. So why should they. When it comes to I any conversation Let them say what they have to say and say youll try to do better If their wrong you still say sorry, because why) Because what ever words you say wont change their ══════> minds, But saying youll do better will be something theyll not be able to argue with, but you gotta actually do it, not just say it. So just let them say what they have to say, you cant change how they think no matter what so deall with it, dont argue even If their rong, you cant change what the think say your sorry youll do better then theirs no fight, nothing you said that was stupid that you regret, so just chill let it go and take note and try harder.

125

TEACHING MIKEY
FOUND by Molly Eyres

NONE OF US ARE GAY
FOUND by Paul McCarthy

Aaron

~~Tonight Tonite~~

Tonight's event was just a tradition of the house. It was not gay even though you had to pull down your pants. At least you didn't have to show it to all the actives! Just your pledge master.. Its meaning = To prove your manhood and that you are not a boy. You swear we want to see your dick! Everyone has done it but none of us are gay.

Aside from all this, I want you to know that I be seen some improvement out of you

#265

since you 1st pledged. Keep up the effort and have a positive attitude of things. I tell ya, its all worth it once you cease! Take my word for it! Just hang in there ok? I want you to have dinner w, me when you are free someday. Its a great dance for you to get to know me better and for me to answer questions. You may have. alright?

Good shit lil'bro.

A.J. Wilson

#265

ETT

"This is one page from some kind of pledge journal found outside a fraternity house at the University of California, Berkeley." **Paul**

Inbox for ████████@yahoo.com
powered by hp

Yahoo! - My Yahoo! Options - Sign Out - Help

✉ Mail Addresses Calendar Notepad

Reply | Reply All | Forward | Inline text ▼

Delete | - Choose Folder - ▼ | Move

Flag This Message

Prev | N

Mark as

Download A
Printable View - F

| Block Address | Add to Address Book

Message-----
From: ████████
[mailto:████████]
Sent: Wednesday, May 15, 2002 10:05 AM
To: ████████@hotmail.com';
████████@hotmail.com';
████████@hotmail.com'; ████████@hot
████████@hotmail.com';
████████.com';
████████@hotmail.com';
████████@hotmail.com'; ████████.com
████████.com'; ████████@hotmail

Subject: The dish...

The update

Well...Mr. Colin ████████ showed up at my door at about 8:15ish. Sporting a pair of cute jeans, a button up and a black jacket. As for looks, he was cute but on the shorter side and his hair was a little too long. Far from a mullet but longer than I would prefer but let's not dwell on that because he can kinda get away with it. So for looks, I would probably give him another B. Car- BMW, like I stated before. A great car, he'll have to get and A for that. He gets and A+ for his manners and politeness. Marcie, he opened the car door everytime! Super polite. Overall general appearance will cap at a B+.

AS for the place we went to, another "A". The Tasting Room is an excellent date place. I was never the wine connoisseur but I'm gradually thinking I could become one. We had 4 glasses each of different white wines and a cheese flight, which was the perfect food mecca to go with the wine. Place is awesome, I recommend all of you guys to attend this place for a night out with your man/woman. We also headed over to this place called the Black Duck. Another great place! The date place itself gets an overall "A".

By the way Girls, this summer we must hang out on Randolph, so many awesome places!

I can go into great detail of what we talked about and such but, that would make for an extremely long email.

The date ended with me getting intoxicated but not like crazy intoxicated, but I was drunk. No hangovers. I'm assuming he was fairly intoxicated but since he was driving, I didn't want to know, so I never asked.

By the way, as for myself, I get an overall A+ for how damn cute I looked. I sported a pair of fun longer Capri pants from Guess in a darker khaki color with my white shirt from Hanger 18, that has my lower back showing with my new cute fitted black jacket with empire sleeves from Armani. I was a BABE. He didn't stand a chance. My worries of not being cute were so swept under the rug with the outfit I pulled off last night.

Before jumping to any conclusions, YES, I stayed the night, only because I semi passed out on his couch and he was polite to ask if I wanted to head home and I just said he could take me home in the morning, NOTHING happened. Honestly only a kiss derived from this date and it didn't even happen at his place. I believe it might have been executed at the Black Duck but I'm not so sure on the exact time and location. But can I add, GREAT kisser. The date kiss gets an "A". Really, I haven't had that great of a kiss since, well we won't go there but it has been a long time. I might have to go with the fact that I might have mastered the skill of French kissing, no joke. As long as I have potential to work with, I can execute a pretty intense kiss.

Lara- you would have loved Colin's attitude. Actually I think all of would have appreciated how he called me out on my stupid logic of thinking.

Somehow, it came up on how random it was for us to meet and shit and how when he said the very first time we talked for me to give him a call and my response was, "Really, I'll let you know now, I won't call you, so I suggest you write my number down and give me a call". Hence the wait of a week or so for his first initial call was due to my shallowness or whatever you would like to call my way of playing the field. Doesn't really matter, he still called and I didn't.

So, question is, where do I stand on the whole outlook of Mr. Colin and the date... The car, the money, the job, the cute apartment, the boat-which by the way only seats 6 people, so I really don't consider that really amazing, his mannerism and his great kiss will probably lock in another date but...I can tell you now unless he cuts his hair and sends me gifts, it won't lead me to seek anything more than my 1st 30 year old FRIEND (Oh by the way, I think he's only 29, but still, I'm rounding up). Plus, the summer is just around the corner and guys are EVERYWHERE, I need to keep the options open and my schedule free to lock in some other great summer flings...

Well, I hope you've enjoyed the day in the life of Miss Jackie███ and please feel free to comment on my date, my outfit, the kiss, or whatever else. If you need any more major details of the date please contact me in one of the following ways: phone, email, personal visit or text messaging.

Oh, I might be heading to a Cubs game with him next week. We'll see.

Oh by the way ladies- His cute friend Brian, is single and also a day trader. Which by the way, being a day trader is pretty money, literally in a sense but he gets to throw on lounge wear for work and is home no later than Noon. Are you kidding me? Where was being a day trader on career day in Elementary school?

Dear Lyle

Listen to me I just came back from planned pa:
because I wanted to make sure that your nasty
god that I was good and I didn't have nothing
mandatory that they give female pregnany test
positive and they gave me a sonagram and I'm
have a baby on the way and look if it was up
you 'r not gonna have anything to do with 1
and all I feel you have the right to know bu
to get around in this little ass town that I'm p
feel it can't happen because you pulled out.
happened, and it is is very possible for a fen
what you call precum and it can get a fema
and you took that chance and now look w
can do this and be mature about it and d
that me and you hate eachother and we c.
will be the best mistake of my life so list
and you and not the whole god dam I tha
reguardless and I feel that the best thing
parential rights to the baby and nobody
sorry I never thought that this would've l.
getting past this and so these 9 mounths th
know that this is your baby I'll make sure
touch with you and all you gotta do is go
before you know it and
We can go on with our lives. So please d
tell non of your little friends and just ke
Don't say anything to anyone because I
when the time comes when I have the b
johnson ave in Riverdale N.Y. so I'll hol
Fed into all the bullshit but you know wl
best for you and not what other people th

P.S.

Listen you know what when we was in yo
sweet you went to the store for me and b
nice person and deep down inside you're
the wrong people that's all and I'm not ma
got a baby on the way and you need to ge

130

Dear Santa Claus

I am waiting to you for my two Children,
I can not give them Anything for Christmas.
I am a Single parent and hardly make
my paycheck last until the next one.
My Family does not know how hard it
is for me And I would never want
them to know, I don't want to
disappoint them on Christmas. Kimberly
is 12 and Kristopher is 10 yrs old they
are good kids. Can you please help me
give my children something for Christmas
Anything you can give will be greatly appreciated
by us all,

Thank you

DEAR SANTA
FOUND by Megan Reed

"I found a whole folder of letters to Santa Claus behind an
old desk in my office. I hope some of the Christmas wishes
were fulfilled." **Megan**

Dear Mr. Teacher,
I was thinking of you over the weekend. So I have made up my mine to let you in on my thoughts.
First you know that I am married and anything I do that comes first! Now I like older men maybe that's because I am mature ,but I must have order in everything that I do. If you have not thought of me in this way that's fine we can go on as if I never wrote you. If you have then please read on.
I am not as innocent as you may think, or is it that when you look at me, you can tell that I am not so innocent. If that is the case then lets state the things that we know I am 26, I go to school everyday for 2 to 4 hours a day. I love my husband and always want to be with him, but growing up around all males have made me a little selfish, it also has allow me to know my worth and that nothing is for free. But if you are a woman something's you can get away with.
If we are going to spend time together then there are a few rules that must be followed, and something's you need to know about me. The rules first, because you may not want to deal with me after you hear the rules.
Rule #1 You are never allow to call me so I must have a way of getting in touch with you.
Rule #2 You would never see my family.
Rule #3 You must know that it is a privilege to be with me ,for I have picked you for the purpose of fulfilling some of my needs that are not getting satisfied.
Rule #4 Understand that I am looking for some one to spend time with, maybe go to a movie, maybe just someone to talk to. But not a man to be my man. I have one of them already.
Rule #5 If we ever decide to have sex then I will only have sex in a hotel, you will have to pay for the room.(I will never be able to spend the night, but what ever time I spend with you it will always be worth it!)
Rule #6 Everything I do must have order there for meeting up with you will always have to be planed. You must also know that I may have to brake plans. But not likely.
Now, things I feel that you should know about me. I have been married almost 8 years, he takes care of me and his children.

MR TEACHER
FOUND by Ben Zarawski

I have only been with 5 men in my life my husband was my 4th. I have had an affair one time that was about a year a go. It lasted a while but his feeling got in the way. So I had to end something that went on for over a few years. Now if you feel that I am a hoe then we need not get together. I know that I am not a hoe. If we was to have sex I would feel the need to know how many people you are having sex with not because I am jealous but because I am married and you already know who I am sleeping with. I will tell you if I start to sleep with any one else. (Not likely) But in the case that I feel that you are having sex with too many people I will end it. Not because I am jealous but because I am married, and I don't want to bring anything home. You will know more than my husband about my sex life. That's because you will be fulfilling things that he dose not.

Now, may be you think I wont be able to handle you , but the truth is I hope not, I hope there are things that you can teach me for I am willing to learn. If not I hope you are not unwilling to learn what I like. Because I am a big girl and I do know what I like. I am not afraid to let people know what I like. I like to do things and I like to have it done to me. If you are unwilling to do the things I like , then there is no need to get together. For the truth is its all about me, And if YOU want to please me. For in return you will always be please!

I also like to smoke weed most of the time before sex, or throughout sex it helps to relax me if you can't be around it that's fine but never ask me to not smoke. I will never have sex if I am not relaxed.

I know that I have given you a lot to think about. Therefore I will not ask you about this letter. You will have to make the first move . I don't know if you feel the same , or if you are willing to follow the rules(the rules must be kept.) I hope that it something that you will think hard and long about. Please don't start something you can't handle.

One of your students
I am a black female in one of you're a.m. classes.

P.S. I am not doing this to better my grade I am passing your class I got an A on the midterm if you think you know who I am call me into your office and we can talk about it. Tell no one I have just as much to loss as you. May be that's why I picked you. J.A.

"While walking in the hall on a 10-minute break from my college art class I found this zesty little note." **Ben**

Justin Gatlieb

Betsy Ross sewed the first american flag.

George washington was the first american president.

George washington was a general in the war.

martin luther king was a civil rights leader.

Chris columbus discovered America.

George washington ~~cut~~ cut down his fathers cherry tree with an axe his father gave to him for his birthday.

The ~~Black~~ Black Panther was started During the Vietnam war.

the sputnik satellite was launched

man went ~~~~ to outer space

Malcolm X began His Quest for Freedom

The ~~~~ constitution was sighned

The Boston tea party Happened

the anti ~~~~ government group, the anarchy was started.

King Tuts tomb was discovered

the stop light was invented

the 1967 ford mustang shelby was introduced

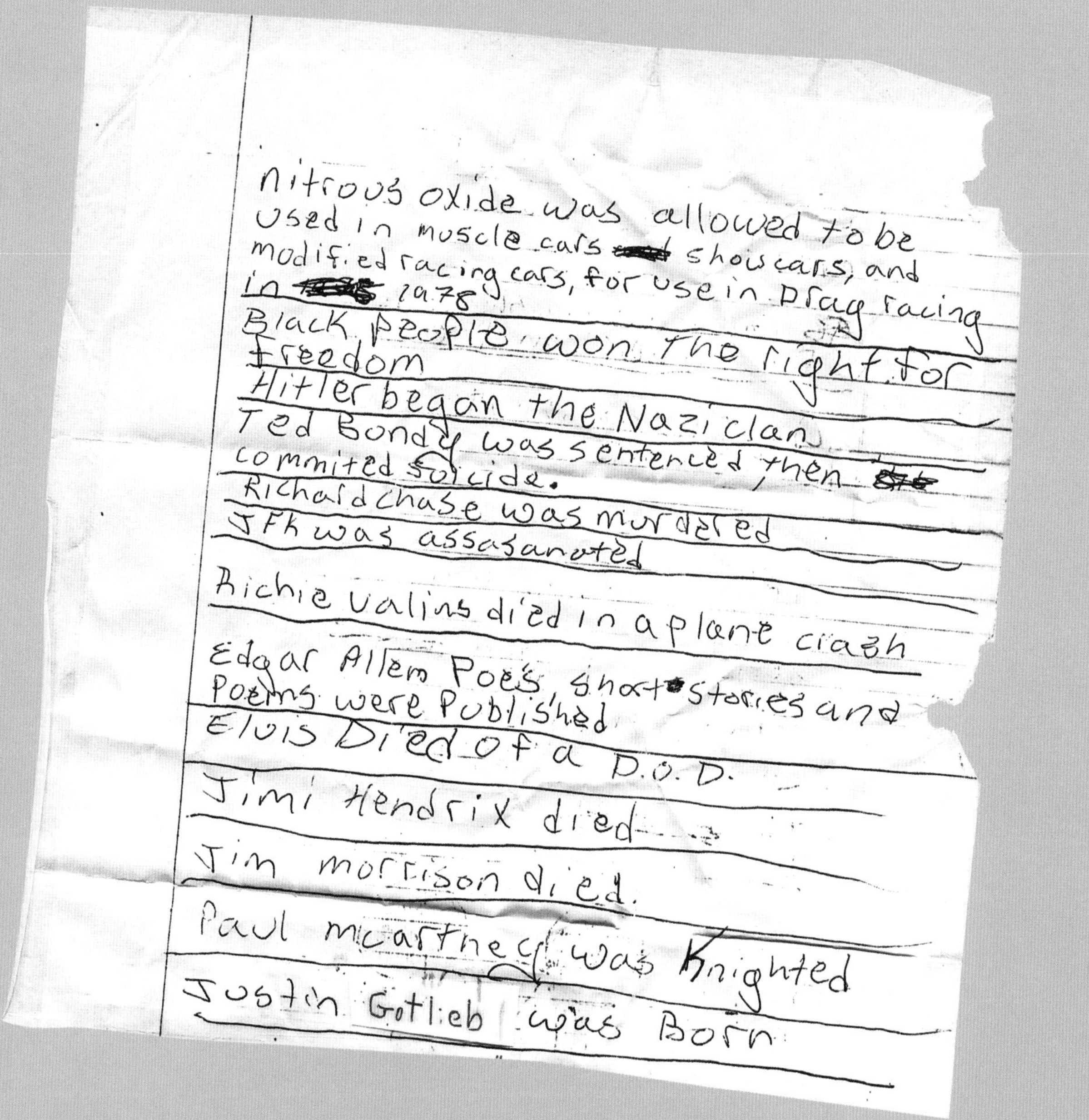

nitrous oxide was allowed to be
used in muscle cars ~~and~~ show cars, and
modified racing cars, for use in Drag racing
in ~~1975~~ 1978

Black People won the right for
Freedom

Hitler began the Nazi clan

Ted Bondy was sentenced then ~~86~~
commited suicide.

Richard chase was murdered

JFk was assassanated

Richie Valins died in a plane crash

Edgar Allem Poe's short stories and
poems were Published

Elvis Died of a D.O.D.

Jimi Hendrix died

Jim morrison died.

Paul mcartney was Knighted

Justin Gotlieb was Born

WHAT I KNOW
FOUND by Rona Miller

ON THE GRILL
FOUND by R.J. Sidwell

RICE
FOUND by Karen Cutter

THEY ARE COMING
FOUND by Brande "Short Line" Wix

257) Will make love in a car

258) Looking for plain, old fashioned security

259) Immensley attracted to me physically by the tone of my voice, the scent of my perfume, the touch of my skin when our hands accidently brush

260) Must be patient, understanding and easy-going

261) Doesn't care how long it takes to bring me to the state of sexual extasy that his own sexual natures crave

262) loyal and loving partner, someone who values security

263) Truly believes that best relationships are often those which takes longer to start off but become more and more contented as the years go by.

264) Who is independent but unlikely to stray for the sake of a fling with someone else.

265) Gentle, caring honest soul who truly believes in the sanctity of home and marriage, of permanent relationships, of living happily ever after.

279) Does not have the Peter Pan syndrome
280) Determined to get what he wants
281) Does not settle for someone he dosen't feel will be there for keeps
282) Enjoys a challeng
283) Not a loner
284) Loving father, uncle etc.
285) Leave no stone unturned to discover what is going to make me happy
286) Be able to turn my gloomy moments into laughter
287) Does not rush headlong into a relationship without thinking about the morrow
288) Senses what makes me tick
289) Not selfish in bed
290) Takes care of his responsibilities
291) Hates the idea of break ups and divorce
292)

"Found this in a copy machine. I'm amazed by the idea of such a list going up to 291!" **Jerry**

AUTION !!
DOOR WILL SWING
OPEN AND NAIL
YOU!

INSTRUCTIONS
FOUND by Lenny Bass

"Found this in an alley, taped to a homemade bong." **Lenny**

Smoking Instructions

1) Suck hard & light bowl on fire until chamber is thick with white smoke. →
2) Exhale **1st** Hit
3) Lock Valve at intake
4) Relax, Tell a Story
5) Unlock Valve at intake
6) Clear Chamber
7) Repeat if Necessary
8) Make Food !!!

PRIORITIES
FOUND by Elizabeth Schnell

Non-Party Things to Do:

✓ Pick haircolor for Amy
· Devise plan for world peace
· Host Post-Party ND / Board Game Party
· get Manicures
· Sew button on to coat

Hey Poochini,
I have missed you today cause
you are so sweet to sniff and
so nice to look at. I will give
you kisses for dinner
cause I cant get enough
of your sweetness. Sorry I am
being silly, you're silly too
though. Yogurt would be
a good thing to eat today
I think, or there is also
chai chocolate, both
would benifit our mouths
& tummies. Some might say
you are my hunny bear
but I would say your are
my lovely poodle. I want
to rub cheeks (face & butt)
because yours are so soft &
warm, and I want to kiss
your jaw spot, the one that
makes me squeel like a little
ninny noo nooo. = I just
made that up. Remember

RUBBING CHEEKS
FOUND by Scott and
Acacia Cocking

142

when I got all that spicy gum and I couldn't stop eating it, not even to save my own mouth, how silly was that!!

REBEL
FOUND by Miriam

144

JUNE 21, 2002

STAN

I am sorry things have turned out so badly.
I will write you a long letter once settled
since
At the moment I have no home.
Give me two weeks.
It would never have been my intention to
hurt you.
"Maureen" is nice and would have been an
excellent
partner for us. She is helping me now in
crisis.
I will always love you despite what you may
believe.

(Jill)

♡

Jill,
Our last present:
Hearts to match the ring we shared.
Burn inscent on glass above candle.

My counselor said you are being cruel in your methods.
Getting dumped I can eventually handle, but it is the
WHY? that I need to know. I need this to
heal and move on.
   Something strictly between your ears?
   OR something I could possibly have done?

At all points, I was open to listen, to talk,
to compromise, to improve → to worship you.

Now, I go home to burn the photos and cry one
last time. The pictures show such intense Love
for three months.

What on earth went WRONG?

Stan
7-18-02

Stan

This relationship and friendship is completely over.

Stop ... Harassing ME!

or I will get a restraining order.

Jill

August 14, 2002

Basically I am here to refute the Petitioner's statement. However:
Whatever the outcome of this court appearance—I will NOT be contacting
or communicating with Jill ____. I would have just let this court date go
by, but for the inaccuracies written in her complaint form.
   After all is known, I feel I have done fairly well for someone alone
and sick in an empty house . Was it realistic for me to just disappear without
the comfort of knowing why this whole nightmare was necessary? After two
months, I have discovered that I really don't care anymore. The answer is
obvious, my heart just had some trouble catching up to my brain. My final
thoughts of Jill are "thank you for the best three months of my life".

I FEEL A RESTRAINING ORDER IS NOT NECESSARY OR JUSTIFIED
Based on some minor lapses which I freely admit.

At no time was I controlling, violent, verbally abusive, stalking or dangerous
To Jill in any way.

Jill,
☐ yes Why? Because I fell for some one else
☐ yes ☐ no I just fell out of Love
☐ yes ☐ no I just wanted to delay, or date
☐ yes ☐ no I just wanted to delay, or date

Other short reason ~~~~~~~~

I did nothing so mean to you that you left so coldly.
Any man in America would have tossed you out with
that hair-brain story. You are a Lost Battle on the waves.

WHAT WENT WRONG?
FOUND by Marlin Florida
continues over the page

continues over the page

145

1) THREW ALL MY BELONGINGS OUTSIDE

I placed her boxes on carefully spread out plywood against my house and under the roof. Jill received all she wanted plus was given access to my home without my Presence. The alternative would be to let her moving group scatter all over my house Not knowing what items belonged to who. Very stressful time that would have been! By the way, she brought her new boy friend right to my home. I was not controlling, Verbal or violent in any way.

2) VOICE MAIL

No messages were ever threatening, controlling, or violent in any way. I was sinking into depression and told Jill my counselor and I would be greatly helped if we were given a reason for her to so abruptly tear my heart in half. She wrote that she would Do this but never did. My notes left on her car refer to this promise. I needed to understand in order to heal. I wanted to avoid future mistakes. I needed closure To move on with my life.

As for the pornographic message— Jill often requested me to leave sexy fake messages from fictitious companies. She loved it!

Another call explained that I was going to drive to California and meet some mutual friends and would she like to come along?

With Jill not responding it was hard for me to adjust. My heart led me to wishful Thinking, and thoughts of her last note of love to me. If Jill had been honest and direct, I would not have bothered her.

My counselor referred to Jill as "unnecessarily cruel". Also stating that Jill is as water seeking its own level. I perhaps was too normal for her. I was "Bonafied" with a job, benefits and yuppy desires. Of course, the counselor stated that She is free to do as she pleases, but that her behavior has been bazaar, callous and cold. I now know that I could never depend on her, but will always feel that I was the best man For her. Jill and I have never really argued or ever really raised our voices to each other. She has no reason to be afraid of me.

3) THE NOTE ON EMPLOYER'S DOOR

This was her personal calendar that SHE highlighted our special days together. I simply circled my birthday, vacation times etc. and encouraged a romantic response.

4) BAG WITH PRESENT LEFT ON CAR

About July 18, I left a romantic present on her car at work. I had completed my vacation without her and happened to see something that matched a ring I had purchased for her previously. Remember, I was experiencing the effects of deep depression until I could find The right medicine that works for my body during July and was experimenting with Prosac (which did not work). My heart held onto 1% hope of reuniting. Her response in a letter was that I had harrassed her. She did mention a Restraining Order. This runs opposite of her speech and letter of June 21—my only two notes from her during all this period of turmoil. I needed answers for my peace of mind, and hopefully to get her to look into the mirror and think better. My notes were asking for common sense, respect and compassion. They were NOT threatening.

5) MAIL TO WORK PLACE

I simply forwarded a letter from Sears to Jill at her office. Jill 's boss led me to believe that possibly Jill had quit that job. I wrote, "If not here-send to circus". This was an inside Joke meant only for Jill . Her boss "involved" herself and proceeded to write copious sour messages all over two personal letters from me To Jill —returning them unopened. The letters contained requests to peacefully Meet and finalize, clarify what is going on. I offered to chat with the new man In her life also.

6) NOTE ON CAR AT Jill 'S APARTMENT

I did NOT follow Jill anytime or anywhere. It is also perfectly legal for anybody To print ADDRESS CORRECTION REQUESTED on a letter, and the new address will Be sent back to the sender for a small fee. However, I knew approximately where Jill Resided and simply looked for her car.

I left my final note asking, "Why did you leave?) This was about 7PM July 29. I never would have driven that far from my home (Woodinville is about 65 miles South) But just happened to be going by on my way to Bellingham. As I pulled back onto the Freeway I noticed that I did not feel good about what I had just done. After more thinking I realized that I no longer cared for her answer—it did not/would not matter to me anymore. I was happy to know that I was finally healing. I made a mental note to pull the Note off her car on my way back home. When that time came, I chose to be a BRAT and Kept driving.

I AM TRULY SORRY FOR THIS, AND SINCERELY APPOLOGIZE TO Jill , AND TO THE COURT.

Due to modern medicine and counseling, I am just pulling out of a deep and momentous depression as of August 6. The color is coming back into my life again.
The key basic facts that I feel are vital are:

1) Jill has not seen me since her move out day of June 18.
2) I was broken hearted and clinically depressed
3) My heart and mind were pulling in opposite directions
4) I failed to act maturely by writing that last note.
5) I will not be going near Jill , her car, her job, her apartment for the next millennium. No phone, No letters, No nothing.

COREY
FOUND by Jessica Mikuliak

TO DO

- email Corey
- introduce him to lesbians
- continue to convince self that I'm not madly in love w/him

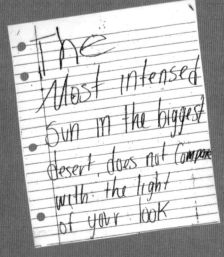

The Most intensed sun in the biggest desert, does not compare with the light of your look

LIGHT OF YOUR LOOK
FOUND by Andrea Gin

"Don't wrack your mind trying to compose that perfect love note – use this one." **Davy**

148

CHOCOLATE STRAWBERRIES
FOUND by Anna Parker

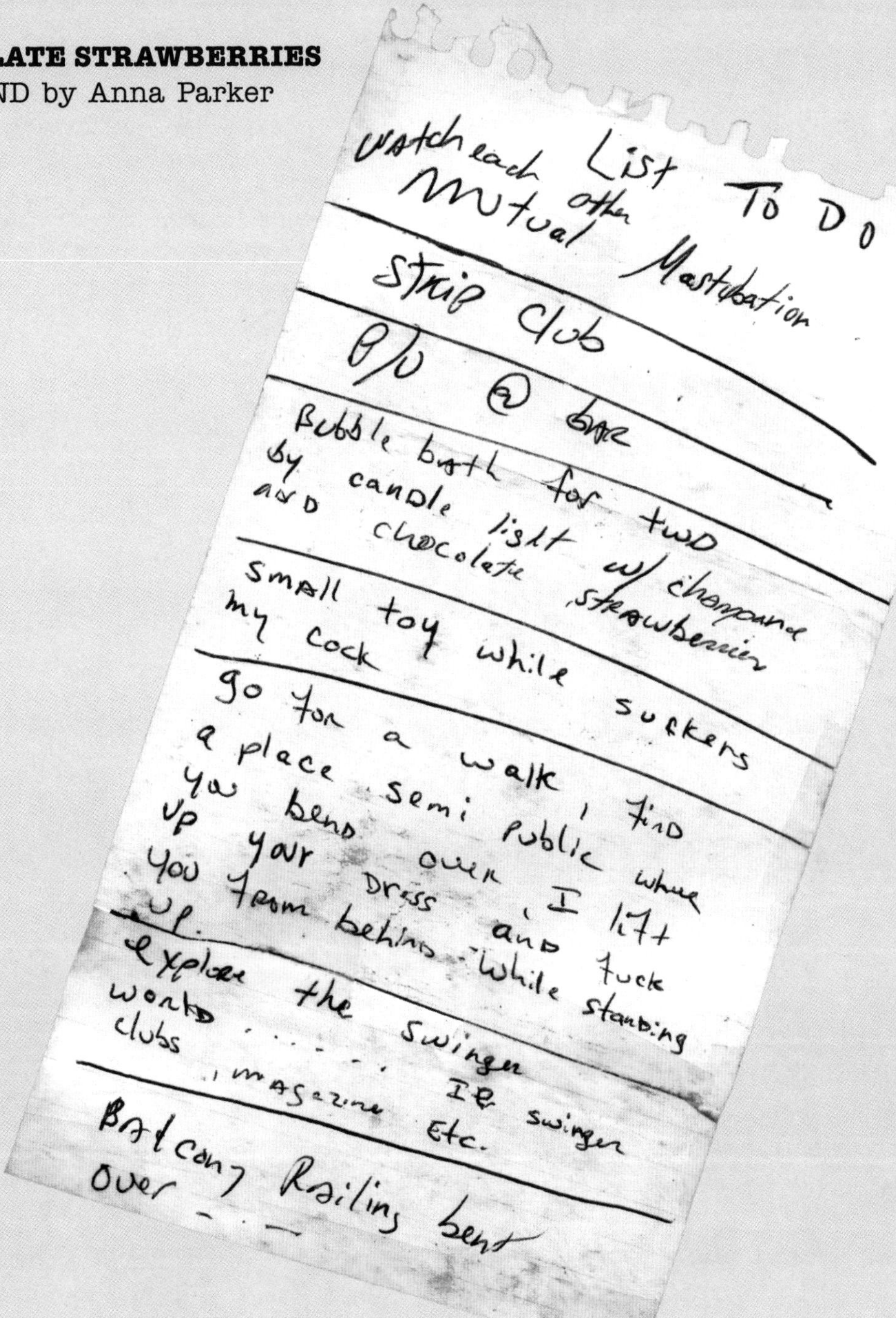

List TO DO

watch each other Mutual Masturbation

Strip Club

B/J @ bar

Bubble bath for two by candle light w/ champagne and chocolate strawberries

small toy while my cock suckers

go for a walk, find a place semi public where you bend over, I lift up your dress and fuck you from behind while standing up.

explore the swinger world ...... IE swinger clubs, magazine etc.

Balcony Railing bent over ___

UNDER GROWN ESCORT
SERVICE

SEEKing DESPRATE WOMAN
TO ESCORT. RICH WEATHY
MEN AROWNO TOWN
ALSO WE ARE LOOKING
For STRIPERS. AMO PRIVET
DAMCERS.FOR VERY PRIVET
PARTYS. FOR MORE
IMFORMATION CALL
MR. ANTHONY GARZA
ON MY BEPPER 1524 8(
OR MY MESSAGE BEPPER
1800 489 70   PEN 58.
LEAVE NAME BRIHE
MESSAGE WITH PHOME NUMBOR
AND WE WELL GCT RBHT BACIC
TO YOU

ALL RIGHT
FOUND by Gretchen Ames

ALEC BALDWIN
FOUND by Jhone Daniels

TALK ABOUT JESUS
FOUND by Scot Nobles
and Jimmy

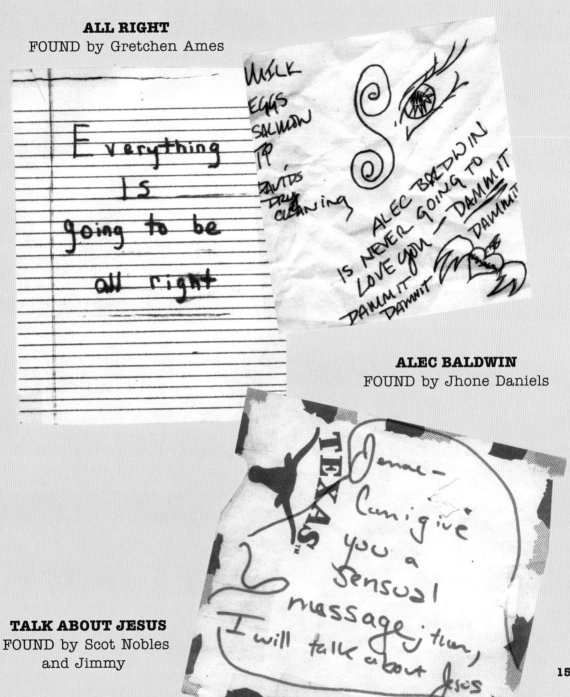

NOTHING BUT THE TRUTH
FOUND by Jeff Brown

1118 Jefferson, St.
Savannah, Ga.
April,18,1928

Dear Sweetheart,

Mildred, will you please tell me whether you love me or not. As you know I am graduating this year. Our principal asked me to go away and study to be a Priest.I told him that Iwould asked my daddy. I did asked him and he said that I could go if I wanted to.Mildred I have always loved you and I always will. If you really love me I will not go, because if I tell the principal yes, Ican not see you for ten years. So please Mildred, tell me "yes " or "no ". TELL ME NOTHING BUT THE TRUTH?

Your loving sweetheart

P. S.   DON'T   FORGET   NOTHING BUT THE TRUTH.

CODE WORDS Monica-Erin
Courtney-Heather

Fish Crackers- zits
M.B- make-up bitch
Flo-up- butt ugly
sotu- slut of the universe
ducats- money
cherry- really fine
I.B- faithful, loyal
smack- lets talk
sheeky- low down
keepin- down low
boink fest- getting it on
golden- special
monet- cute from far away
spicy- tacky
~~bubblegum~~- mad
thrashed- hurt
rock- the bomb
~~pinky~~- matching
chocolate- flirt
foul- stinky
$3 bill- poser or fake

MONET
FOUND by Trevor Harris

(1/24/01)

Hi Dad what's up. Not much here just working
To save money. I'm working at old country Buff
starting at $6.50 an Hour 'Cooking' Dad is there
any cooking jobs down there Let me know when
you write me back. I gave Robert your Letter ok.
without mom knowing, ok. I can't wait to come down
there. Erie sucks bad there ain't nothing to do too
cold the weather sucks too. Dad I drink too beer
Budweiser, but I don't drink alot and I do a
Little drugs too I smoke joints and I got bowl that
is cool I'll Let you see it ok. I talk to
grandma chapman she said that she going to send
you a Letter and some money. Dad I don't know if
Robert or Jill is coming 'down' but I'll talk to
them and see. if not it will just be me only

Dad your going to rent a mobile Home that's cheap
hundred a week that's cheap. Dad try to see if
there's any apment's for rent and Let me know
how much ok. Dad I'm going to take a greyhound
because it's cheap only $49 dollars but you to call
ahead of time. Dad all of the money I'm saveing
from working at my job and my income tax check
I should have a Lot ok with the money we should
be able to get a places for us ok! Dad I can't

wait to come down there pretty soon.

TURN OVER ↘

HI DAD, WHAT'S UP
FOUND by Raspberry Rosen

Dad I'm a cook I can cook some shit up
cook some meals up for us get a grill and cook on that
Also I got a lot c'ds Like AcSDC, Led Zeppelin
over kill, metallica, pink floyed, The Doors,
Jimmy Hendrix, Judus Priest, black sabbath. And all
kinds. And we can Jam out and have lots of fun.

(important Dad)

I'm going to send you some stamps so you
can wright me back and I'm going give you a calling
card so you can call me.

Dad when you get your place give me your
address and let me know where your at.
I miss you and I can't wait to see
you we will have lots of fun

Keep in touch so I know what's
going on ok.

Dad I'm still comeing down there
I can't wait
So let me know what's
going on ok. I love you!
Take care and
Take it easy. ok. Dad
W/B/S!!

"This letter was found in the street after a rain;
its envelope was addressed to a man in Arizona.
I count it among the most moving and affecting
FOUND notes I've seen." **Davy**

155

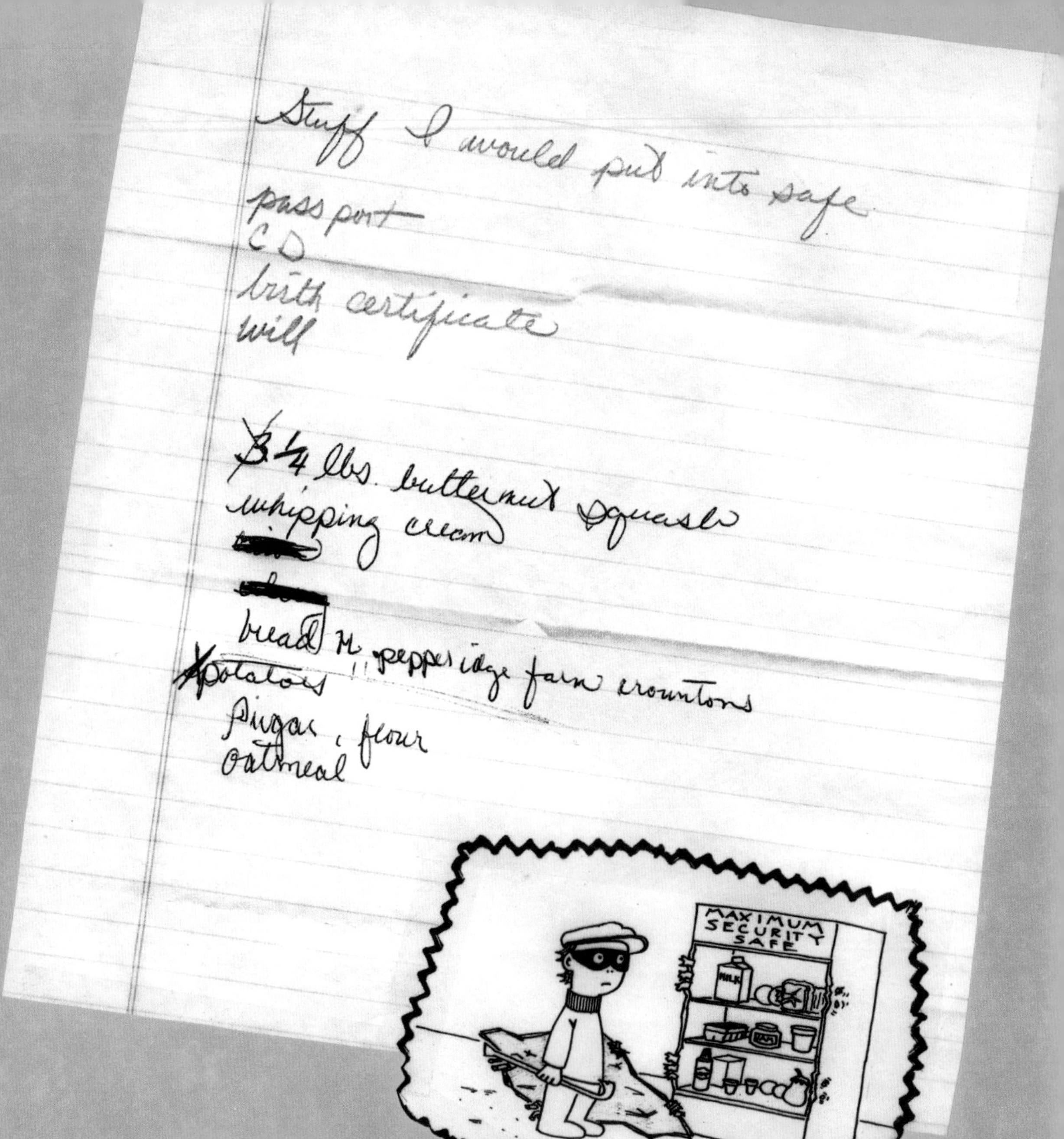

Stuff I would put into safe

passport
CD
birth certificate
will

3/4 lbs. butternut squash
whipping cream
~~two~~
~~bun~~
bread " pepperidge farm croutons
~~potatoes~~
sugar, flour
oatmeal

KEEP SAFE!
FOUND by Jainee

STOLED MY GRIL
FOUND by Kevin and Alyson Seconds

JACK AND DUANE
FOUND by Kathy Block

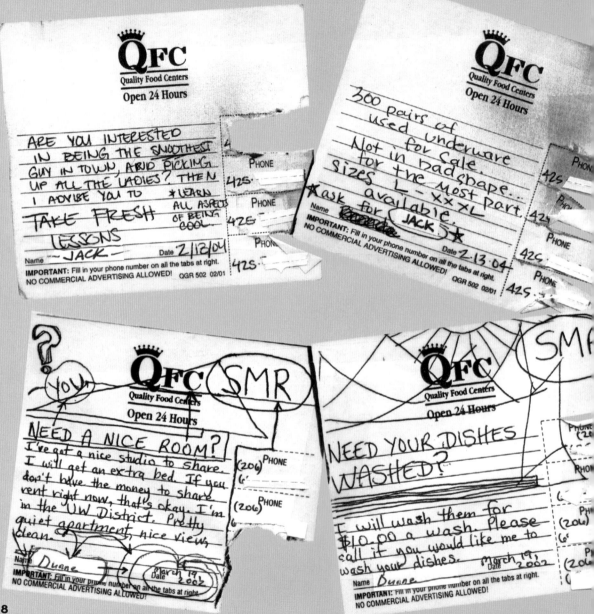

ARE YOU INTERESTED IN BEING THE SMOOTHEST GUY IN TOWN, AND PICKING UP ALL THE LADIES? THEN I ADVISE YOU TO *LEARN ALL ASPECTS OF BEING COOL. TAKE FRESH LESSONS

Name — JACK — Date 2/12/04

300 pairs of used underware for sale. Not in bad shape... for the most part. Sizes L - XXXL available. *ask for JACK

Date 2-13-04

NEED A NICE ROOM?
I've got a nice studio to share. I will get an extra bed. If you don't have the money to share rent right now, that's okay. I'm in the UW District. Pretty quiet apartment, nice view, clean.

Name Duane   March 19, 2002

NEED YOUR DISHES WASHED?
I will wash them for $10.00 a wash. Please call it you would like me to wash your dishes.

March 19, 2002
Name Duane

ANSWERS
FOUND by Ross Drummond

"Some of the questions that inspired these answers are possible to deduce; the others mystify me." **Davy**

Journal Jan 14, 2005

1) I would name my twins Mickey and Miney.

2) Hell no, I mean if your gonna control the U.S armed Forces they you have to be born and raised here in the U.S.

3) The book would be about the ghettos of the world and the title would be "The ghettos of the world."

4) Set my arms on fire using Rubbing alchohol or spitting flames using rubbing alchohol.

5) Nothing at all.

6) I love you God, Jesus SAVED ME.

RIGHT BACK
FOUND by Jonas Westover

BE RIGHT BACK.
— GODOT

MAY 1978

THANK YOU
FOUND by Phil Hassett

Dear Mother and Father,
I feel that somehow I should thank you. But I don't know how, so I suppose I shall save this letter until I do.